Discovering *the* JOY *of a* Clear Conscience

CHRISTOPHER ASH

P&R
PUBLISHING
P.O. BOX 817 • PHILLIPSBURG • NEW JERSEY 08865-0817

First published in the UK by Inter-Varsity Press in 2012 under the title *Pure Joy: Rediscover Your Conscience*

North American edition issued 2014 by P&R Publishing

ISBN: 978-1-59638-703-4 (pbk)
ISBN: 978-1-59638-704-1 (ePub)
ISBN: 978-1-59638-705-8 (Mobi)

Printed in the United States of America

Library of Congress Control Number: 2013919002

How refreshing to see a thoughtful and richly biblical book on the conscience. Christopher Ash performs a vital service for the church by opening up God's truth about this neglected and therefore misunderstood area of biblical truth. The conscience shines light into the darkest corners of the heart, thus facilitating God's people to "guard the heart with diligence" (Prov. 4:23).

—*Tedd Tripp, Pastor, Author, and Conference Speaker*

Christopher Ash has done us a great service in writing *Discovering the Joy of a Clear Conscience*. After serving as a pastor and biblical counselor for twenty-seven years now, I found myself saying, 'Yes, this is exactly what so many people are struggling with.' In a world that questions absolute truth and mocks any sense of right or wrong, people are being left shattered in a wake of confusion and hurt, unsure what to think and wondering why they feel so bad about so many things. Christopher points us back to our God-given conscience but is careful to explain how unreliable it is apart from the Word of God. *Discovering the Joy of a Clear Conscience* gives a simple and biblical path that can lead confused, hurting, and guilt-ridden people back to the grace of God and the hope of the gospel. This study of the conscience is also a great resource to better understand how God calls us to exercise Christian liberty without trampling over the law of love. I think this book will serve as a useful guide to Christians looking for more personal joy, as well as to the community of believers who want to love each other in the midst of diversity. Read this book and pass it on to others!

—*Brad Bigney, Senior Pastor, Grace Fellowship Church, Florence, Kentucky*

Discovering the Joy of a Clear Conscience will attune you to your own inner voice of conscience, as well as revealing its limitations and showing how you can bring your conscience more in sync with God's will. It's great to see this neglected area being so helpfully explained, and I'm sure this book will be a blessing to many people.

—*Tim Chester, Leader, The Crowded House; Director, Porterbrook Seminary*

This rare treatment of a complex practical issue shines clear biblical light into the dark areas of our thought and behaviour, with lucidity and great pastoral relevance. It will make you think and do you good. I warmly commend it.

—*David J. Jackman, Former President of the Proclamation Trust*

In an age when so much attention is paid to our physical well-being, here is a liberating and nourishing book that addresses the urgent need of our souls. Whether we are haunted by past failure, paralysed by sinful habits, hardened by disobedience, or longing for the joyful freedom of a conscience cleansed and a life lived by God's grace, we all need to engage with this timely book.

—*Jonathan Lamb, Director, Langham Preaching; Chairman, Keswick Ministries*

Over the past few decades, we have witnessed a revival of expository biblical teaching in our churches. Now we need a renaissance of biblically shaped pastoral care and counsel which takes that Word into the furthest corners of the human heart. Of course we can still learn from, and integrate, the best that psychology and psychiatry have to teach us. But the pages of Scripture rustle with insights into the human 'heart' and with 'cures' for the aching soul. Christopher Ash's book on conscience, full of practical wisdom and advice, is an important stepping stone towards realizing this vision. I hope it will inspire and equip a new generation of 'doctors of the soul'.

—*Glynn Harrison, Professor Emeritus of Psychiatry, University of Bristol, UK*

Few things are worse than a troubled conscience. Christopher Ash peels back the layers to understand the mysteries of the human conscience. *Discovering the Joy of a Clear Conscience* will help you to be happy inside, inviting you to come to Christ and enjoy the warmth of his sunshine. This book doesn't just take the reader for a suntan, for skin-deep spirituality, but aims to shine the light of Christ all the way down to our conscience.

—*Dave Bish, UCCF Team Leader*

To my dear parents,
who showed me what a
healthy conscience looks like

CONTENTS

ACKNOWLEDGMENTS

I TRIED OUT EARLY DRAFTS of parts of this material on students at the PT Cornhill Training Course, preachers at the Irish Preachers Conference, members of the congregation of Emmanuel, Wimbledon, students from Eden Baptist Church in Cambridge, and the summer congregation of Burry Green Chapel in South Wales. I am grateful to them all for their encouragement.

I am thankful to all those who read and commented on drafts of the manuscript, including my patient wife Carolyn, Stephen and Zoë Moore, Robin Weekes and my editor Eleanor Trotter. I am especially grateful to Nicole Carter and Professor Glynn Harrison for major suggestions and insights, and most of all to Ursula Weekes for going through the whole manuscript with a fine-toothed comb and making a great many perceptive and observant comments and suggestions. My thanks also to Erica Tapp for practical help.

As authors always say, the end result is my responsibility. But it is a lot better for these insights from others.

INTRODUCTION: CLEAN INSIDE!

DO YOU FEEL CLEAN INSIDE? Do you know the joy of a clear conscience? If you die today and have time for some final words, will you be able to say, 'I have nothing bad on my conscience; I can face whatever comes after death with confidence and not fear, because I know my conscience is clear'? It is a wonderful thing to be able to say that, not only today, but every day.

But how can this be possible without self-deception, fooling myself that I am OK when I am patently not? And how can I say this without self-righteousness, conceitedly setting myself up above the common run of messed-up people? Well, it is possible, wonderfully possible. But it is only the good news of Jesus Christ that can enable any of us to enjoy a clear conscience with honesty, integrity and thankfulness.

This book is about the joy of a clear conscience in every day of living and in the day of death. In *The Pilgrim's Progress*, John Bunyan uses the crossing of the River Jordan as a picture of the transition from this life into the life to come. He says of one of his characters, Mr Honest, that 'in his lifetime' he 'had spoken to one *Good-conscience* to meet him' on the banks of the Jordan, which he did, 'and lent him his hand, and so helped him over'.[1] In real life, others too have known such an experience. A close friend of mine knew he was dying of cancer and wanted, as he put it, 'to die well'. It was a good ambition, and he did die well; he died with a clean conscience.

But it is not just in dying that we need a clean conscience; it is also in living. One wise old writer said that conscience is either the greatest friend or the greatest enemy in the world.[2] We shall need to think about both possibilities. Someone else said that a good conscience makes everything taste sweeter. With a good conscience we can enjoy not just the stuff we think of as 'spiritual', but all sorts of things like sleep, sport, friendship and holidays. When we have a good conscience none of these things ever leaves a sour taste in our mouths. This same writer said that a good conscience can even sweeten times of trouble. 'The conscience,' he wrote, 'is God's echo of peace to the soul: in life, in death, in judgment it is unspeakable comfort.'[3]

This book is an invitation to a journey of rediscovery, to think quietly about your conscience, to listen to what the Bible has to say about it, and to reach the point where you can say each morning and evening, 'I have a clear conscience.' Whether or not you call yourself a Christian, I want to invite you on this journey. Read the book slowly and give yourself time to think about the questions at the end of each chapter. Because your conscience is something inside you, only you can examine it. No-one else can go on this journey for you, although it may be helpful to meet up with others on the same journey in order to compare notes. The questions at the end of each chapter should help to focus your thinking, either as you consider them alone or in discussion with others.

This book is in four parts. In the first three chapters, part 1, we take a look at what conscience is. We shall see that, paradoxically, this inner voice is at the same time unreliable and indispensable. In part 2, we think about conscience as symptom: what does my conscience, and in particular a guilty conscience, tell me about myself? Part 3 looks at the choice my conscience faces me with: how shall I respond to the experience of a guilty conscience? Finally, part 4 comes back to the question of conscience as guide, looking at it now from the viewpoint of someone who knows the blessing of full and free forgiveness.

The stories in the book are fictional (unless there is a footnote to show otherwise), but I hope they are not unrealistic.

May God bless you as you embark upon a journey which may well be life-changing.

Notes

1. John Bunyan, *The Pilgrim's Progress* (Penguin, 1965), p. 370.
2. Richard Sibbes, *Works* (James Nichol, 1862), vol. VII, p. 490.
3. William Fenner, quoted in J. I. Packer, *Among God's Giants: The Puritan Vision of the Christian Life* (Kingsway, 1991), p. 150.

PART 1
CONSCIENCE AS GUIDE

1

THE INNER VOICE

'I knew it was the right thing to do.'
'I feel awful about what I said to her.'
'I have written this email to him. But part of me feels it would be wrong to send it.'
'Don't do that. You know it would be wrong.'

NONE OF THESE SPEAKERS uses the word *conscience*. But each one is talking about it. It is a neglected word. If we think about it at all, it may be in the context of 'prisoners of conscience', men and women in prison because they refuse to compromise on what is a matter of conscience for them: admirable yes, but it seems far removed from most of our experience. Or perhaps we think of some great 'issue of conscience' in medical ethics or Parliament. Or in history we may come across 'conscientious objectors' who refused to fight at a time of war. In short, conscience feels like the stuff of exceptional cases.

But what about the idea that each of us should examine our consciences as part of the daily discipline of life? This is not something that many of us take seriously today. My aim is to get you thinking about your conscience again. I want you to take it out of the cupboard, dust it off, bring it back into daily life and rediscover its power to do you good.

So what exactly is the conscience? Here are three ingredients which together help us to understand what the Bible means by conscience.

What does conscience mean?

Self-awareness

At the lowest level, conscience means an awareness of myself. It is very similar to consciousness, that uniquely human ability for 'I' to think about 'me'. This is the origin of the word. *Conscience* is a word that came into English from Latin. It means something like a knowledge ('. . . science') that is shared ('con . . . ', meaning 'with'). The family of Greek words translated as 'conscience' in the New Testament have the same origin: the main word is *syneidēsis*, where *eidēsis* means 'knowledge' and *syn* means 'with, or shared'. The Old English word (technically Middle English) was *inwit*, where *wit* means something like 'knowledge' or 'judgment' (rather as we speak about our wits) and *in* points to the inwardness of it. At the most basic level, conscience means an inward knowledge, a self-awareness, a knowledge shared inwardly with myself. It is to do with self-knowledge.

Moral self-awareness

But the meaning of a word comes not just from its origins.[1] Both in the New Testament and also in English, conscience has the sense not just of self-awareness, but of *moral* self-awareness, an awareness within myself about right and wrong. So the *Oxford English Dictionary* begins one of the meanings of the word as follows:

> The internal acknowledgement or recognition of the moral
> quality of one's motives and actions; the sense of right and
> wrong as regards things for which one is responsible . . .

The New Testament includes this sense in its use of the word.

There is no separate word for *conscience* in the Old Testament, but the idea is still there and is often expressed by the word *heart*, which includes this intellectual dimension. Conscience makes me aware in my mind that *this* is right and *that* is wrong. Conscience takes the universal principles of right and wrong that I know, and applies them to my particular circumstances. For example, I know it is right to honour my parents. So, when my elderly parents need me to do some shopping for them, my conscience deduces for me that it would be right to help them if I can. That is a trivial example. Others are much more difficult, especially when there seems to be a clash of obligations. Conscience begins with thinking about what would be right to do, with making reasoned judgments about what is right and wrong behaviour.

Moral self-awareness that touches my affections and my will

But conscience is more than merely intellectual. The *Oxford English Dictionary* definition continues by describing conscience as 'the faculty or principle which pronounces upon the moral quality of one's actions or motives, approving the right and condemning the wrong'.

As well as helping me know the right thing to do, my conscience makes me feel bad if I do the wrong thing and feel at peace if I do the right thing. It makes me averse to wrong and drives me towards good. It touches my affections and my will. We all know what it is to feel bad about having done something we believe to be wrong or to feel good about something we did that was right. Conscience is not just a logical conclusion; it exerts a moral force and may even be thought of as a kind of voice inside me, 'telling' me what to do. That is why this chapter is headed 'the inner voice'.

One of the ways in which conscience does this is by making me feel that my knowledge of right and wrong is shared. In particular I feel that it is shared with God: I know this particular thing would be wrong, and God knows that I know it would be wrong. This gives to my conscience a particular force. The Bible uses it in this sense, as something God has placed within human beings to give them a sense of right and wrong. The apostle Peter uses the word in this sense when he writes to Christian slaves that 'it is commendable if someone bears up under the pain of unjust suffering because they are conscious of God' (literally, 'they have conscience of God' or, as one commentator puts it, 'for conscience toward God'[2]) (1 Peter 2:19); they bear up because they know it is the right thing to do. Augustine spoke of it as 'the inner part of man in relation to God', whether it be 'man's religious organ, man's antenna into the divine sphere, the hub of man's readiness to receive impulses from the supernatural and the transcendent, [or] man's divine nucleus.'[3]

The theologian J. I. Packer writes that for the sixteenth-century Reformers, 'Conscience signified a man's knowledge of himself as standing in God's presence (*coram Deo* in Luther's Latin phrase), subject to God's word and exposed to the judgment of God's law.'[4] Milton described it in his poem *Paradise Lost* as God's 'umpire' within people.[5]

We shall take conscience to include all three of these elements. It is a self-awareness, a reflective faculty within myself that enables me to reflect upon myself. Specifically, it enables me to think about the rightness or wrongness of my words, actions and thoughts. And, because I have some sense that this awareness of right and wrong may have something to do with God, it tends to make me averse to wrong and want to do right. That is to say, it pushes or pulls my will. It is my inner voice.

It is helpful to focus on some specific features of conscience.

Five features of conscience

1. *Conscience speaks with a voice that is independent of me*

> 'I want to buy that car, but I feel uneasy about whether it would be right.'
> 'I really enjoyed that relationship, but something inside me feels wrong about it.'

Notice about this self-awareness that these feelings seem to be – at least to some extent – independent of me. That is to say, I get them when I don't want them. Suppose for the sake of example that I am thinking of doing something really selfish with my money. I have just received an inheritance, or a bonus from my work, and I am thinking of using all of it to buy something I want, something that is completely unnecessary and entirely self-centred. I really want this item. And yet I find something like a little voice inside me saying, 'Isn't that a really selfish thing to do? Don't you think there is something better you could do with the money? You could give some of it away, or share it with your family, you know.' I don't want to hear that little voice. Frankly, it annoys me. And yet it is there. J. I. Packer says that 'conscience is largely autonomous in its operation. . . . It normally speaks independently of our will, and sometimes, indeed, contrary to our will. And when it speaks, it is in a strange way distinct from us.'[6]

Conscience can be a very powerful and unsettling voice. Guilty criminals have given themselves up to the police because of conscience. Political prisoners have endured torture because of it. Guilt-ridden individuals have been driven to despair because of it. Martyrs have faced death with joy because of conscience. Here is a voice that we cannot ignore.

2. *Conscience speaks with a voice that looks forwards and backwards*

> 'I wish I hadn't told that lie. I feel so awful about it now.'
> 'It would be so much easier to tell that little lie. But something inside me tells me I oughtn't to do it.'

Secondly, this tiresome little 'voice' (if we may call it that) speaks to me both about things I have already done and about things I am thinking of doing. Looking backwards, it passes an internal judgment upon the past, telling me that this was right or that was wrong. But it doesn't wait to speak until I have decided and acted; it begins speaking to me while I am in the process of deciding, reasoning and arguing with me that this would be the right thing to do or that would be the wrong thing to do. It both passes retrospective judgments and also acts as a guide for future choices.

3. *Other people can appeal to my conscience*

> 'Sure. You can walk out on me. But you know very well it's the wrong thing to do.'
> 'It's a hard call, I know, and it will cost you a lot. But you know it's the right thing to do.'

Other people know that the little voice is there inside me. And sometimes they appeal to it against me. 'You know that would be wrong,' they say, despite my having told them I propose to do it. Or they may say, 'You knew it was wrong', contradicting my attempts to justify my action. They appeal to what I 'know' (that is, 'know' in my conscience) against what I actually do, or have done, and what I say. My conscience is like a disloyal part of my own army, ready to fight against me when it disagrees with me and to make my life miserable when I disagree with it.

So when Paul is teaching the church in Rome to honour the civil authorities, he says, 'it is necessary to submit to the authorities, not only because of possible punishment but also as a matter of conscience', or as we might paraphrase it, 'because you know it's the right thing to do' (Romans 13:5).

There is an almost light-hearted little example of this in the Old Testament book of Ecclesiastes, one of the so-called 'Wisdom Books' of the Bible. Here the wise man says to us: 'Do not pay attention to every word people say, or you may

My conscience is like a disloyal part of my own army, ready to fight against me when it disagrees with me and to make my life miserable when I disagree with it.

hear your servant cursing you' (Ecclesiastes 7:21). Most of us don't have servants today, but we understand what he is saying. Don't listen at the keyhole. Don't peek at their emails. Don't look at their Facebook pages or what they tweet. If you do, you will probably hear them say some unflattering things about you. The friend who smiles sweetly when she meets you for coffee may say bad things about you to her boyfriend later. If you get to hear it, you will be upset.

So we ask, why shouldn't I listen in to the conversations of others? Here is the answer: ' . . . for you know in your heart that many times you yourself have cursed others.' The expression 'you know in your heart' means pretty much the same as 'your conscience tells you . . . ', 'you are aware within yourself that . . . '. You know, if you are honest with yourself, that there are plenty of times when you have smiled sweetly at someone while behind their back saying some pretty bad things about them. And maybe you are their friend, up to a point. You know that you don't always mean what you say, or not as strongly as you say it. So remember that other people are just like you. Just as they probably don't fully mean the things they say to your face, so they may not fully mean all the nasty things they have said behind your back. So when I am getting on my high horse, indignant about that nasty thing someone said about me, the writer appeals to 'what I know in my heart' to persuade me to get off my high horse and admit that I'm not as consistent as all that myself.

We need to remember that, although someone may appeal to what they suppose we 'know' to be right or wrong, we may not agree with them. 'I'm glad Osama bin Laden was killed the way he was,' says someone, 'I know it was the right thing for someone to do.' But another person may have misgivings and not be so sure. (We will be thinking more in later chapters about what happens when your conscience and my conscience disagree.)

4. God can appeal to my conscience

A man was once asked to write an essay about a great preacher. He thought about people like John the Baptist or the apostle Peter, or some of the great figures of church history such as George Whitefield or John Chrysostom. But in the end he wrote about 'another preacher, known in all the corners of the earth, heard by every generation since the creation of man, one who has access into kings' palaces and behind locked doors. And the preacher he wrote about was Conscience.'[7]

The Bible says that God appeals to our consciences. There is a vivid example of this in the book of Isaiah. To persuade the people they are in the wrong, Isaiah tells a story about a farmer who planted a vineyard. The soil was good and all the preparations were exemplary. But the grapes were sour. So whose fault was it? It wasn't the farmer's fault. The problem was the bad quality of the vines.

After telling the story, Isaiah says,

> Now you dwellers in Jerusalem and people of Judah,
>   judge between me and my vineyard.

What more could have been done for my vineyard
  than I have done for it?
When I looked for good grapes,
  why did it yield only bad?
(Isaiah 5:3–4)

The hearers of the story are invited to pass judgment in favour of the vineyard farmer and against the vineyard; clearly, they are supposed to say, the fault lay with the vineyard rather than with the farmer.

But then at the end of the account we discover that the vineyard in the story is the people who are listening (Isaiah 5:7). God is appealing to them to pass judgment against themselves! He is saying, 'Admit that I'm in the right and you are in the wrong. Make the judgment against yourselves.' He is appealing to what they know to be right in their hearts; to their consciences. 'You know you're in the wrong; your consciences tell you that, even though you don't want to admit it, so stop pretending you're in the right.'

Thomas Aquinas called conscience 'a man's judgment of himself, in line with God's judgment of him'. The Puritans spoke of conscience as more than this, indeed as God's watchman and spokesman in the soul, 'God's spy in our bosoms', 'God's sergeant he employs to arrest the sinner', 'God's deputy and vice-regent within us'. We shall have to look carefully at the question of whether conscience is the voice of God or not.

5. I do not need a Bible to hear the voice of my conscience

Here is an extract from a conversation about a criminal trial:

'It wasn't his fault. He never had parents to tell him it was wrong to do what he did. His dysfunctional childhood and social deprivation meant he didn't know it was wrong.'

'You don't need parents to know that it was wrong. Everybody knows that rape is wrong.'

Another feature of these feelings is that they are not – or not entirely – dependent on somebody telling me what is right and what is wrong. At least some of the time, I don't need a law code from God to know that something is wrong. For example, we rather assume that everybody everywhere knows that murder, rape and kidnapping are wrong.

In his letter to the Romans, Paul writes about some Gentiles 'who do not have the law' – that is, the law of Moses, the Ten Commandments, and so on – and yet do at least some of the things required by the law, 'their consciences also bearing witness, and their thoughts sometimes accusing them and at other times even defending them' (Romans 2:14–15).[8] They do have a conscience, even if they don't have the biblical law.

In the Bible we see this in two ways. First, we see it among God's people in the period before God gave them the Ten Commandments. For the first part of the Bible story (from the start through to Exodus 20), God hasn't given people any laws. Well, that's not quite true. In the garden in Eden (in Genesis 2 and 3), he does tell Adam not to eat the fruit of one particular tree (Genesis 2:16–17). But apart from that, there aren't really any laws, and there is certainly no law code that spells it out in detail. And yet even in that early time, the Bible suggests that people had some sense of right and wrong.

A classic example is when Joseph was a slave in Egypt. He has been promoted to be household manager for a rich Egyptian called Potiphar. Potiphar is away from the house during the day on business and he leaves Joseph in charge. And then Potiphar's sexually frustrated wife tries to seduce him. Joseph refuses, saying, 'How . . . could I do such a wicked thing and sin against God?' (Genesis 39:9). Joseph knows it would be wrong. His conscience tells him. How does he know? You may say perhaps he knew because Egyptian law codes told him, or because in his childhood his parents had told him. Both of those may be true, and probably are. The influence of parents on the early formation of our consciences is very significant indeed.[9] But it still leaves the question of how law codes or parents knew it was wrong. Later we shall need to look closer at how our consciences are formed and the role of culture and upbringing in shaping them, but for the moment let's just note that this inner moral voice seems to be present, at least to some extent, in everybody, and has been throughout history. As Christians would say, conscience is part of the residue of the image of God in humankind.

The second way the Bible speaks of this sense of right and wrong is by condemning foreign nations for their evil. A classic example of this is at the start of the prophecy of Amos. The first two chapters take a tour of the nations around the edge of God's people Israel, telling us what they've done and why they must be punished. So, for example, the people of the Philistine city of Gaza 'took captive whole communities and sold them to Edom'. They captured a whole ethnic group and sold them as slaves. And so they must be punished. Then Edom is condemned for warfare, for slaughtering men and women, 'because his anger raged continually and his fury flamed unchecked'. In our terms, he used disproportionate force. Ammon is condemned because he 'ripped open the pregnant women of Gilead in order to extend his borders'. In our terms, they waged offensive war and committed war crimes. The point is that none of these nations had been given the Ten Commandments. But they didn't need them to tell them that these kinds of things were wrong. They knew they were wrong; their consciences told them they were wrong, and so they could quite fairly be punished for doing them.

We will return later to this question of the extent to which everybody knows right from wrong when we think about how our consciences can be distorted, hardened and even brutalized. And it is sadly true that some people have been so traumatized, and are so dysfunctional because they have been abused, that their consciences hardly seem to operate at all. But for the moment the point is that, even for these people, there is some vestige left of a sense of right and wrong.

So what is conscience?

Conscience is our self-awareness, particularly about right and wrong. It is the faculty within us that enables us to distinguish between them. It pushes us away from wrong and pulls us towards right. It is a voice within us that can speak with a strange independence from us. It looks both forwards and backwards. Others can appeal to it when trying to persuade us to behave well. And repeatedly in the Bible God himself appeals to it. Although we shall see later that our consciences are not reliable, there is a residual sense in which we have a conscience, whether or not we have a Bible.

Questions for personal study or discussion

1. What experience do you have of your conscience making you feel clean and good about something you have done? Try to think of specific examples.

2. When has your conscience made you feel awkward or uneasy about something you are thinking of saying or doing? Again, think of particular examples.

3. Have you ever appealed to someone else's conscience to persuade them to do, or not to do, something? Can you think of examples?

4. Do you agree that everybody has a conscience, however they were brought up and whatever their culture?

5. Do you think that conscience is the voice of God within you? Why? Or why not?

Notes

1. This is to say, etymology (a word's derivation) cannot determine meaning. For example, a 'cupboard' is not a 'board' upon which you may put a 'cup', even if it may once have meant that.
2. E. G. Selwyn, *The First Epistle of St. Peter* (Macmillan, 1969), p. 176.
3. Philip Bosman, *Conscience in Philo and Paul* (Mohr Siebeck, 2003), p. 17.
4. J. I. Packer, *Among God's Giants: The Puritan Vision of the Christian Life* (Kingsway, 1991), p. 141.
5. John Milton, *Paradise Lost*, Book III, lines 194–195: 'And I will place within them as a guide my Umpire *Conscience*.'
6. Packer, *Among God's Giants*, p. 144.
7. David Watson, *Know Yourself* (IVP, 1964), p. 3.
8. These are a difficult pair of verses. For another understanding of them see Christopher Ash, *Teaching Romans* (Christian Focus, 2009), vol. I, pp. 101–104; or, for a more technical discussion of the Greek, C. E. B. Cranfield, *Romans*, International Critical Commentary (T. & T. Clark, 1975), vol. I, pp. 159–163.
9. Freud noted this, and although he overstated it, it is still true.

2

THE UNRELIABLE VOICE

Sue and Hikari are talking on the phone.

Sue: 'I know you disapprove of what I am doing and think it's wrong. All I can say is that I have searched my conscience and it seems and feels right to me. So I am sure it is OK and you don't need to worry. After all, I'm sure you'd agree that I must be guided by my conscience. Wouldn't you?'

Hikari pauses . . .

MY CONSCIENCE, as we have seen, may be thought of as my inner voice. But whose voice is it? Could this be the voice of God inside me? We need to think carefully about this.[1]

Always let your conscience be your guide?

If you've seen Disney's *Pinocchio* as a child, you will remember the little figure Jiminy Cricket who is Pinocchio's conscience. You may remember (or may even be able to sing) the song that he sings to Pinocchio called 'Give A Little Whistle!'. Jiminy Cricket says that whenever Pinocchio is unsure about what's right and what's wrong he should whistle for him to come and advise him. The punchline is the famous phrase: 'Always let your conscience be your guide.'

But is that punchline right? *Always* let your conscience be your guide? Always? Is what I 'know' to be right always right? Is what I feel is wrong always wrong? And what about when my conscience gives different answers from your conscience? What should Hikari say to Sue?

We've seen already that we all know what it is to feel bad about having done something we know to be wrong, or to feel bad when we are thinking of doing something we know to be wrong. And we all know the good feeling of reckoning we did the right thing, and the good – almost heroic – feeling of thinking about doing the right thing.

Where do these feelings come from? How reliable are my feelings when it comes to right and wrong? And what about when we appeal to these feelings in others and say things like 'Go on. Do it. You *know* it's the right thing' or 'Don't do that. You *know* it's wrong'? Why do they 'know' it's right or wrong? How do I know that they know? What if they tell me that really they don't know or agree with this at all? And so on. All of this boils down to the key question: 'How reliable is conscience? Is it in any sense the voice of God inside us?'

To help us, we're going to focus on two important truths.

Conscience is an unreliable guide

I want us to understand one thing, that *conscience is an unreliable guide*. There's a surprising and revealing little section in Paul's first letter to the church at Corinth, at the start of chapter 4.

In this passage Paul is defending his apostleship to the church, where his genuineness has been called into question. He says he has been entrusted with the gospel, and so the key thing is that he be faithful or trustworthy (verses 1–2). But is he faithful? Is he an authentic minister of Christ, or is he an imposter, a charlatan? And who is to judge? That is the issue at stake.

Paul begins his answer by saying, 'I care very little if I am judged by you or by any human court' (1 Corinthians 4:3). It is easy to see the logic of this. You have no window into my soul, he says. You cannot therefore judge the motives and intentions of my heart. You have no infallible means of knowing whether or not I am genuine in what I say. So in the last analysis I do not care what you think! This is not very polite, but it is logical and intelligible.

But what he says next is very surprising: 'Indeed, I do not even judge myself' (1 Corinthians 4:3). 'But why on earth not?' is the question we want to ask him. I can see that I cannot judge your heart, because it is your heart and not my heart. But surely you can judge your own heart. You do not need a window into your own soul, for it is your soul and you live there. If anyone knows what is going on inside you, your hopes, your fears, your motives, your real intentions, it is you, isn't it?

'No,' says Paul, 'ultimately it is not.' So he goes on, 'My conscience is clear [lit. I am not conscious of anything against myself], but that does not make me innocent' (1 Corinthians 4:4).

Here is a very striking claim. 'Do you mean, Paul, that even when your conscience tells you that you have done nothing wrong, you can't be sure you haven't?' 'Yes,' he says, 'that is exactly what I am saying.'

Although it is a right and natural thing, when I have a clear conscience, to say so,[2] it does not prove everything. It shows I think I am in the clear, but it does not prove whether I really am. For there is only one person who has a true and undistorted window into my soul, and it is not me: 'It is the Lord [that is, Jesus] who judges me' (1 Corinthians 4:4).

Paul is a servant and apostle of the Lord Jesus Christ, and only the Lord Jesus can infallibly and accurately judge what is going on in his heart. So, he says, 'Therefore judge nothing before the appointed time; wait until the Lord comes' – that is, until the personal return of the Lord Jesus and the last judgment. 'He will bring to light what is hidden in darkness and will expose the motives of the heart' (1 Corinthians 4:5).

What is going on in your heart and mine is so deep and so dark that you and I are not even reliably informed about it ourselves. Sometimes we realize that we do not know what is going on in our own hearts. There have been times in my life when someone has asked me to express a preference. I say I don't mind at all. And then they take me at my word and make the choice themselves, only for me to realize that I did in fact have a preference after all! The communication line between my self-awareness and the depths of my heart is an unreliable one.

But it's even more serious than that. 'There is a way that appears to be right,' – a course of action that someone's conscience says is all right – 'but in the end it leads to death' (Proverbs 14:12). So I can do something that seems and feels right to me and still end up under the judgment of God. Just because it feels right doesn't mean it is right.

When the first human being sinned, the human race became so deeply twisted that the link between the heart and the mind became corrupted. Our inner

Our inner wiring is full of wrong connections; we do not even understand our own hearts.

wiring is full of wrong connections; we do not even understand our own hearts. 'The heart is deceitful above all things and beyond cure. Who can understand it?' (Jeremiah 17:9).[3]

There is a revealing example of this in New Testament days, in Ephesus. Paul writes twice to the church leader Timothy, who is struggling to deal with some wrong teachers. Paul says two apparently contradictory things about these people. First, he says that they have 'rejected' 'a good conscience' (1 Timothy 1:19)—they did things they knew to be wrong. But then later he describes them as people who are self-deceived (2 Timothy 3:13)—the things they once knew to be wrong they have now persuaded themselves are right after all. Conscience is a delicate instrument and it becomes distorted. In the end we no longer feel things to be wrong, even though they are.

We must not be over-optimistic about how accurately conscience works. The Bible says that sometimes a culture will distort conscience so much that people will 'call evil good and good evil . . . put darkness for light and light for darkness . . . put bitter for sweet and sweet for bitter' (Isaiah 5:20). A conscience can become so twisted that it is not just inaccurate; it is even reversed.

Being guided by my conscience is like trying to decide where I am using a GPS whose satellites are all in misaligned orbits. Sometimes I feel something is OK when it's not, and sometimes I may think something is not OK when actually it is. So conscience is an unreliable guide and Jiminy Cricket is not completely right; we should not always let conscience be our guide.

Just as I may *feel* healthy when I am actually suffering from the early stages of some terrible malignant and progressive disease, and I may *feel* very ill when suffering from a cold (especially a man-cold), so my feelings may not be reliable indicators of my objective medical condition. Conscience is not the voice of God.

We need to bear in mind a couple of health warnings. Here they are.

Health warning 1: you may think you are innocent when you are guilty

In chapter 4 we will be piecing together a portrait of a guilty conscience, what it looks and feels like. You *may* find yourself thinking, 'Well, this looks pretty awful. But happily I don't really feel like this. So I guess I must be OK.' The warning is this: just as you may feel medically fine when actually you are suffering from a terminal disease (as yet undiagnosed), in the same way, you may not be experiencing the symptoms of a guilty conscience and yet be guilty. There is such a thing as false assurance, thinking I am OK when I'm not. Beware a shallow complacency.

Health warning 2: you may think you are guilty when you have been forgiven

The second health warning is the other side of the coin. Just as there is such a thing as false assurance, so also there is such a thing as coming under false condemnation. The Bible teaches that there is a devil, also called Satan, the one who loves to level accusations at real Christians. In Revelation 12:10 he is called 'the accuser' of Christians. If you are a real Christian, and you feel terrible after reading chapter 4, go straight to chapter 7 and read it. (In fact chapter 7 is – by a long shot – the most important one in the whole book. Read and re-read it!)

In his book *Spiritual Depression: Its Causes and Cure*, Martyn Lloyd-Jones writes about real Christians who are dogged by the thought that one particular sin in their past is not forgiven.[4] Somehow they cannot get rid of that feeling of guilt. They pray so much to be released from it, but still it remains. Lloyd-Jones' advice is to stop praying about it! Praying will focus your thoughts on this sin even more. You will be filled with morbid introspection about it. No, don't pray. Instead, stop and think about Christian truth. Think about what Jesus did for you on the cross. Think about the truths of chapter 7. As I was told as a very young Christian, 'For each look within (myself), take ten looks at him (Jesus Christ).'

Depressive illness and distortions of conscience

It is important also to recognize that depressive illness (and certain other psychiatric conditions, such as prolonged grief and obsessional illness) are liable to distort our perceptions of past guilt. Just as we view the future more negatively, with less and less hope, so we are prone to view the past more negatively, feeling exaggerated guilt and finding it hard to receive and enjoy forgiveness. Some of this may go back to our child-hoods. An adult subject to constant criticism as a child may know a sense of guilt and failure as an almost constant experi-ence. We need to be humble about the complexity of the human mind and heart and realize that it may take a long time before the wonder of forgiveness is even partially accepted by a particular person.[5]

There is such a thing as objective right and wrong

We need to be clear about something else. When we think about the unreliability of conscience, there is a danger that we will despair of ever having any grasp of right and wrong. We may even slip towards thinking that right and wrong are purely sub-jective, in other words, what is 'right for me' or 'right for you'.

Describing his childhood and his father's vain attempts to interest him in Christianity by taking him to church at Christmas and Easter, the writer Will Self said this:

> Try as he might to enthuse us with the sonorous beauties of the King James Bible, as declaimed by middle-class, middle-aged men in dresses, it was far too late. We had already been claimed by the split infinitives of *Star Trek*, were already preparing to boldly go into a world where ethics, so far from inhering in the very structure of the cosmos, was a matter of personal taste akin to a designer label, sewn into the inside lining of conscience.[6]

But ethics (right and wrong) is not just a subjective matter of personal taste 'sewn into the inside lining of conscience'. It does exist objectively. Some actions, words and thoughts are right, others are wrong. Just because my GPS is relying on satellites in misaligned orbits does not mean I do not *have* a location! I do have a location, a precise location; my inability to ascertain that location precisely does not mean that it does not exist.

Issues of conscience in Rome and Corinth

In two of the churches to which the apostle Paul wrote, there were issues of conscience causing distress. We will have reason to come back a number of times to how Paul addresses these issues, so it will be good briefly to introduce them here.[7] Neither issue is likely to get our blood racing today. In fact, both seem pretty irrelevant to many of us. But the principles with which the New Testament addresses them are important for us.

The Christians in Corinth had written to Paul to ask him whether or not they should eat food that had been sacrificed to the gods and goddesses of the Greek pantheon (Zeus, Aphrodite, and so on). They asked whether it was OK to buy meat in the marketplace when they were not sure whether the animal had been killed in a pagan sacrifice. What should they do if they were having dinner with a friend and another Christian told them the meat on their plate had been sacrificed to a pagan god or goddess? Most meat available for eating did come from animals killed in this way, so it was an important question. The meat didn't come with a label, 'Sacrificed to the goddess Aphrodite', rather as our packaging might say, 'Contains nuts'! Some of the Christians felt it was wrong to eat this meat; others thought it was fine.

In Rome the issue was different.[8] Some Christians were from a Jewish background, others were Gentiles. The Jewish Christians were used to keeping the kosher food laws and observing the Jewish Sabbath and other religious festivals; the Gentile Christians had never done this. It seems that this was causing tensions. Some of the Jewish Christians felt it right to continue to keep their kitchens kosher and guard the religious days in their diary; others were happy to join the Gentiles in not bothering about these things any more. And each group whispered disparagingly about the other.

So both in Corinth and in Rome the church was divided. Some people's consciences told them it was OK to do something, while other people's consciences told them it was not OK. What was to be done?

There are still debates today about conscience and food. Should non-Hindus living in India eat beef, given that it will cause offence to the consciences of Hindus? Should a school barbecue serve just halal meat if most of the children are Muslim? These contemporary issues give us a feel for the issues in Rome and Corinth.[9]

We will come back to Rome and Corinth in chapters 3 and 8. For the moment I want us to notice one thing: In each case, the apostle Paul makes it clear that there is a right answer. It is not just a question of what is 'right for me' or 'right for you'. Paul does this in three ways.

First, he begins 1 Corinthians 8 with an emphasis on knowledge (verses 1–7). Words to do with knowledge appear nine times in these seven verses. Although Paul is not impressed with the boastful way some of them were trumpeting their 'knowledge', he does not deny that it is true knowledge: 'So then, about eating food sacrificed to idols: we know that "An idol is nothing at all in the world" and that "There is no God but one"' (1 Corinthians 8:4).

We know, he says, that the gods and goddesses of the Greco-Roman pantheons do not objectively exist outside of the imaginations of their worshippers. We know this from what we call the Old Testament (e.g. Deuteronomy 6:4), and Paul agrees; he knows this too. It is a right knowledge. 'But,' he continues, 'not everyone possesses this knowledge' (verse 7).

So Paul begins his argument by agreeing with them that it is possible to know from the Bible that idols have no real existence, that they are the subjective creations of the imaginations of their worshippers. He does not go on to spell this out in 1 Corinthians 8, but the implication is that it doesn't matter for a Christian to eat food sacrificed to these deities, since they do not exist in the first place! So even though people's consciences varied in the verdicts they gave, they were not all right. Some consciences were right in their verdict (it is OK to eat this food), while other consciences were wrong.

Paul makes the same point in a different way in 1 Corinthians 10. He says there that they can 'Eat anything sold in the meat market without raising questions of conscience' (1 Corinthians 10:25), and the reason why they can safely do this is because 'The earth is the Lord's, and everything in it' (1 Corinthians 10:26).

This is a quotation from Psalm 24:1, which teaches the consistent truth that the God of the Bible is the one and only Creator and owner of everything on earth. The meat in question therefore belongs to him, just as 'the cattle on a thousand hills' belong to him (Psalm 50:10). So of course we can eat it. We know this from the Bible, in this case from the Psalms. So there is a right answer, an objective truth that the Bible gives us access to.

In Rome too Paul argues confidently about the truth, although in this case it is from the teachings of Jesus and the apostles in what we now call the New Testament. He says of the food question that 'I am convinced, being fully persuaded in the Lord Jesus, that nothing is unclean in itself' (Romans 14:14) and that 'all food is clean' (Romans 14:20).

He knows this from what Jesus taught about clean and unclean food in Mark 7:14–19, and he agrees with Mark's editorial comment that by this teaching Jesus 'declared all foods clean' (Mark 7:19). And he knows it also from the revelation we now have in Acts 10 and 11, in which the Holy Spirit effectively repeats this same teaching of Jesus and shows the apostle Peter that all foods are now clean and that this abolition of the old food laws symbolizes the abolition of the distinction between Jew and Gentile, so that Gentiles are brought into the people of Christ. Again in Rome, we see that although consciences varied in their conclusions, they were not all right. Some were right (all foods are now clean), others wrong.

The issues were different in Corinth and in Rome. But the principle remains the same. Although our consciences are not reliable, nevertheless Scripture does give us a reliable guide to truth.

Putting this together with the unreliability of conscience, we may think of conscience as a poorly calibrated scientific instrument, a misaligned compass, or kitchen scales that are not properly adjusted. There is such a thing as a true measurement in each case. But our conscience may err. And it may err in one of two directions. It may tell us that something is wrong when in actual fact it is right, or it may tell us that something is right when in actual fact it is wrong. Sometimes my conscience is on one side of God's line, so that it makes me feel things are OK when they are sinful; at other times it may be on the other side of God's line, telling me to keep away from things I could legitimately enjoy or do.

And yet, although our consciences are unreliable, they are the only inner voice that we have. And therefore it is very important that we pay attention to them. Here is the paradox: I must pay careful attention to the unreliable guide inside me, something we now turn to.

Questions for personal study or discussion

1. Have you ever thought that your conscience was the voice of God and later realized that you were wrong?

2. Can you think of examples of an individual's upbringing or culture shaping his or her sense of right and wrong?

3. Why is it not safe to think that being guided by my conscience is all I need to do in life?

Notes

1. In Snapshot 2 of the Appendix we look at some of the ways people have approached this question in history.
2. Paul himself does this in 2 Timothy 1:3 and 2 Corinthians 1:12, and the writer to the Hebrews does it in Hebrews 13:18.
3. Sometimes this is called 'the noetic effect of the fall', that is, the effect of the fall on human thinking.
4. D. M. Lloyd-Jones, *Spiritual Depression: Its Causes and Cure* (Pickering and Inglis, 1965), pp. 66–69.
5. I am grateful to Professor Glynn Harrison for this paragraph. Richard Winter, *The Roots of Sorrow: Reflections on Depression and Hope* (Marshalls, 1985), ch. 12, is helpful on this. Also Michael Lawson, *D is For Depression* (Christian Focus, 2006), pp. 83–84.
6. Will Self, *The Independent Friday Review*, 2 April 1999.
7. The Bible passages are 1 Corinthians 8, 1 Corinthians 10:23–29 and Romans 14:1 – 15:7.
8. I have outlined the issue in more detail in Christopher Ash, *Teaching Romans* (Christian Focus, 2009), vol. 2, pp. 195–233.
9. I am grateful to Ursula Weekes for these contemporary examples.

3

THE INDISPENSABLE
VOICE

Alisha's friends from the church twenties' and thirties' group were going for supper in the pub one Tuesday night. They invited Alisha, who replied, 'That's really kind of you. But I don't think I should come.'

When asked why, she said, 'Well, before I was a Christian, I often used to go to the pub and I usually drank too much, and sometimes I did things afterwards that I now bitterly regret. It doesn't feel right to go. Sorry.'

'Oh, come on!' they said, 'Don't be a spoilsport. We're not going to drink too much. Why don't you come and join us?'

WHAT DO YOU THINK about the example above? Should Alisha go with her friends or not? Alisha's conscience tells her not to ('it doesn't feel right to come'); should she listen to her conscience or not?

Alongside the sobering truth of the last chapter there is a paradoxical counterpoint. Although my conscience can never be one hundred per cent reliable, it is vital that I respect and am led by it. That is to say, I must respect my conscience, even when it is wrong!

Conscience and integrity in Corinth and Rome

Let's return to Corinth and Rome.[1] The next thing we learn from Paul's teaching is that it is vitally important that you and I never do something that our conscience tells us is wrong – even when our conscience is wrong to tell us it is wrong! Although this seems paradoxical, we shall see that it is very important. In the example at the start of the chapter, Alisha would be wrong to go to the pub with her friends if her conscience tells her it would be wrong for her.

We pick up Paul's argument to the Corinthians. He agrees with them that he and they know (correctly) that idols don't objectively exist, and therefore it is objectively OK to eat this meat (1 Corinthians 8:1–7). But the problem is that not everyone knows this – really, inwardly knows it in their consciousness or their conscience. 'Some people are still so accustomed to idols that when they eat sacrificial food *they think of it* as having been sacrificed to a god' (1 Corinthians 8:7, emphasis added).

Imagine a man who four weeks previously had been a regular worshipper at the temple of the goddess Aphrodite. He was at that time an idolater. That is to say, he thought of Aphrodite as real. And in a way she was real – real to him and influential in his life. Her worship played a part in shaping his life. Now he is a Christian. But it will take time for him to unlearn the wrong things that have shaped his life so far. He cannot help thinking of the meat as having been sacrificed to the goddess he used to worship. He has not yet really deeply grasped that she is not a goddess but an idol, not real but imaginary.

Verse 7 continues: ' . . . and since their conscience is weak, it is defiled.' This man has a self-awareness of what is right and wrong. But it is 'weak', young, untutored, inaccurate, and it – wrongly but strongly – makes him feel that it would be wrong to eat this meat. So when he eats it, perhaps urged on by those with 'strong' consciences, the people with the knowledge, his conscience is 'defiled', made dirty.

What has happened is this: he is convinced that Aphrodite exists and that the meat has been offered to her as a goddess. He is therefore convinced that it would be – must be – wrong to eat it. But still he does eat it. He therefore does something which he believes to be wrong, and yet, believing it to be wrong, he still does it. In his heart he is therefore disobedient, setting himself against what he believes is the will of God. He disobeys his conscience, and therefore makes it dirty.

So Paul goes on, speaking to the rather cocky knowledgeable people: 'But food does not bring us near to God; we are no worse if we do not eat, and no better if we do' (verse 8). In other words, although you (the strong ones) are right to say that you can eat this meat, you really don't have to eat it, and it won't do you any harm if you don't. Indeed, there are bigger issues at stake:

> Be careful, however, that the exercise of your rights [the rights that you are so proud of, that you can eat this meat] does not become a stumbling block to the weak. For if someone with a weak conscience sees you, with all your knowledge [true knowledge, but proud knowledge], eating in an idol's temple, won't that person be emboldened to eat what is sacrificed to idols? (1 Corinthians 8:9–10)

But whereas it didn't do you any harm, it will do them harm: 'So this weak brother or sister, for whom Christ died, is destroyed by your knowledge. When you sin against them in this way and wound their weak conscience, you sin against Christ' (verses 11–12).

The language is very strong. By pressuring this weaker brother or sister into doing something they believe to be wrong, you will push them down a path that will ultimately lead to their destruction (as we will see later).

Later in this letter (10:23–33), Paul fills out the picture. But just before this he warns his readers to steer well clear of idolatry (1 Corinthians 10:14–22). Although idols have no real existence,

I can still worship them as if they are real. And when I do that, I make the one true God rightly jealous (verse 22). So, says Paul, when it comes to meat from the meat market, it is absolutely fine to eat anything—for example if you are asked out for a meal with an unbeliever (verse 27). After all, it belongs to God the Creator anyway (verse 26).

He then goes on to address the proud objections of the knowledgeable person, who doesn't like their freedom to be circumscribed by anyone else's conscience:

> But [and it is a big 'But'] if someone says to you, 'This has been offered in sacrifice,' [and the subtext of this comment is a tone of anxiety from someone who is used to thinking of the idol as a god or goddess] then do not eat it, both for the sake of the one who told you and for the sake of conscience. I am referring to the other person's conscience, not yours (verses 28–29).

His key point is that the final salvation of the other person is much more important than whether or not I can enjoy my 'rights'. I must not cause him or her to stumble (verses 31–33).

The principle here is integrity, or what the Old Testament sometimes calls the 'uprightness' or 'purity' of your heart (e.g. Deuteronomy 9:5, translated 'integrity' in NIV). Paul speaks of his conscience testifying that he and Timothy 'have conducted ourselves in the world, and especially in our relations with you, with integrity and godly sincerity' (2 Corinthians 1:12). Actions that are consistent with convictions are the mark of a good conscience.

I must be consistent with my convictions. If I do not do what I believe to be right, or if I do what I believe to be wrong, I cut myself in two, into the person who believes one thing and does another. As James puts it, 'If anyone . . . knows' – that is, knows in their conscience, their convictions – 'the good they ought to do and doesn't do it, it is sin for them' (James 4:17). It is the pure in heart, not the double-minded and inconsistent, who are blessed.

This same principle can be found in Romans 14, which we looked at earlier. The church has one group with one conviction (that the Jewish food and calendar laws no longer apply) and one group with a contrary conviction (that they do still apply). The important thing is that 'each of them should be fully convinced in their own mind' (Romans 14:5); that is to say they should act in accordance with their internal convictions or their conscience (although the word is not used). To pressure someone to act against their convictions and conscience is to put a stumbling block or obstacle in the path of their faith (Romans 14:13). The person who 'has doubts', that is, doubts about the rightness of eating this food, 'is condemned if they eat, because their eating is not from faith', that is to say, it does not come from a heart that really believes this is the right thing to do. And 'everything that does not come from faith is sin' (Romans 14:23). This last statement is saying that anything I do that does not spring from a genuine conviction (faith) that it is the right thing to do, is sinful, compromising my integrity.

This business of personal conviction is so important that 'if anyone regards something as unclean, then for that person it is unclean', even though Paul insists that actually and objectively it is not unclean (verse 14)! So how can something be simultaneously clean and unclean? The answer is that it is objectively clean, since Jesus has declared it to be clean (Mark 7:19); but if a person thinks it is unclean, then for them to eat it would be to damage their integrity as a person, and deliberately to do something they believe to be wrong. And therefore for them, subjectively, it would be unclean. The Puritan Richard Baxter wrote, 'If you forsake [conscience] and go against it, you reject the authority of God, *in doing that which you think he forbids you.*'[2] To do this would reflect a sinful set of the heart, a setting of the heart against God.

This principle of personal conviction and integrity works in a positive way as well. When Paul is writing to Philemon asking him to welcome back someone who has wronged him, he says, 'I did not want to do anything without your consent, so that any

favour you do would not seem forced but would be voluntary'
(Philemon 14). He wants Philemon to be so persuaded that this
is the right thing to do, that he does it voluntarily, rather than
because Paul has pressured him to do it.

In answer to the question, 'Is conscience the voice of God?',
we now find ourselves giving a more nuanced answer. No, it is
not the voice of God in any absolute or universal sense. And yet
it is the voice of God in another sense. The Puritans were right
to regard conscience as more or less the voice of God in the
human heart.

But what if I'm not sure what the Bible teaches?

Jennifer wrote to her new pastor, 'Very sadly I was divorced
some ten years ago. My husband had an affair, and despite
sustained attempts at reconciliation, our marriage ended.
Since then I have become a Christian and have studied what
the Bible teaches about remarriage after divorce. I understand
that some Christians believe the New Testament teaches that
I should remain unmarried if I cannot be reconciled to my
husband. Others think the New Testament teaches that, in the
circumstances of my divorce, it would be all right for me to
marry again. I am not sure what I think. But I don't want to
risk doing something which I think might be wrong. So my
conscience tells me I should remain unmarried.'

How should Jennifer's pastor reply? In Rome and Corinth the
apostle Paul is quite clear as to the truth, the objective truth.
In many of the issues we face, we cannot be quite so sure.
Sometimes it is hard for us to distinguish issues of conscience
from issues of Bible interpretation. And what do we do when
Christians we respect, who believe the Bible is our trustworthy
authority, differ as to what they think it teaches?

This is not easy. We shall come back to it later. The truth we need to emphasize at this stage is that our conscience is intimately related to our integrity. It is very dangerous to do something if I believe (even perhaps tentatively) that it is wrong. I may later come to the settled conviction that the Bible does allow it, but until I reach that settled conviction, I must err on the safe side and follow my conscience.

Questions for personal study or discussion

1. Can you think of any examples of things you once thought to be OK, but which you now know from the Bible are wrong?

2. Can you think of anything you once thought and felt to be wrong, but which you now see the Bible allows?

3. Have there been times in your life when you have allowed yourself to be pressured into saying or doing something you believed to be wrong? What effect did this have on you inside?

4. Have you ever joined with others in putting pressure on someone to do something he or she believed to be wrong?

Notes

1. See ch. 2.
2. Richard Baxter, *Works* (George Virtue, 1838), vol. I, p. 116.

PART 2
CONSCIENCE AS SYMPTOM

4

THE GUILTY CONSCIENCE

To the others in his sports club, Gareth looks like someone who has it all—married with three small children, in a steady job that pays the mortgage, and so on. But unknown to his friends, Gareth is a troubled man. Twenty years earlier, unknown to his parents and everyone else, he had begun sleeping with his girlfriend. He had got her pregnant. They had quietly agreed she should have an abortion (or a 'termination' as it was called to make it seem more impersonal and clinical), which she did.

No one knew except the two of them and the doctor. All quietly dealt with and out of the way, or so he thought. But his (now ex-) girlfriend consequently suffered from severe clinical depression and took her own life five years later. No one knew about the business with Gareth and no one could prove a connection between the two, as Gareth had often said to himself. He wanted to forget the whole sorry episode and move on, but somehow he didn't seem able to. The memories kept creeping back. Hiding his secret began to take its toll and make him bad-tempered and unsettled. His wife could not work out why. It seemed such a strange thing in a happily married man.

You may think that since conscience is an unreliable guide, you and I don't need to be too worried by it. How wrong you would be! My problem is not so much that my conscience is unreliable but that I cannot manage even to keep my own standards. If I could always follow my conscience, that would not make me innocent. But how much more guilty I am when I do not even heed it.

This chapter will be hard reading. We are going to think together about what a guilty conscience feels like and what it does to you or me. In the next chapter we will press this further to ask what a guilty conscience indicates about me.

A story about guilty consciences

Here's an extraordinary story, which is in many ways an object lesson: that of Joseph and his brothers. It has been popularized in recent decades by Andrew Lloyd Webber in his musical *Joseph and the Amazing Technicolor Dreamcoat*. In the original Bible story (Genesis 37 – 50), the drama is driven by guilty consciences.

The family is deeply dysfunctional. The father, Jacob (or Israel), has children by four women (two wives and two concubines). Twelve of these are sons, including Joseph—who, together with his younger brother Benjamin, was a son of Jacob's favourite wife. For various reasons the other, older ten sons hate Joseph with a passion. Again and again in the story, a guilty conscience surfaces in these ten brothers.

A *warning conscience*
The first and second time conscience appears in the narrative, it is to warn the older brothers not to do something wrong. When Joseph is sent by his father to find his ten older brothers in the fields where they are tending the family flocks, they see him coming and one of them suggests they kill him. But Reuben, the

oldest, says, 'Let's not take his life. Don't shed any blood. Throw him into this cistern here in the wilderness, but don't lay a hand on him' (Genesis 37:21–22).

Reuben knows it would be wrong to kill him, and he plans to rescue him later. So they throw him into a cistern alive. And it seems that Reuben goes away, perhaps to find some other flocks of sheep.

While Reuben is away, Joseph is languishing at the bottom of this dried-up well. Then the brothers see a caravan of travelling merchants. At this point Judah says, 'What will we gain if we kill our brother and cover up his blood?' (Genesis 37:26).

When Cain killed Abel back in Genesis 4, Abel's blood 'cried out from the ground' to God. Judah's conscience tells him that the blood of murder cannot really be covered up. Always it cries out to God for punishment. And so Judah suggests they sell Joseph alive into slavery, which they do. Both Reuben and Judah know it would be wrong to kill Joseph.

The guilty conscience of all ten brothers

The brothers sell Joseph into slavery and pretend to their father Jacob that a wild animal has killed him. Even though they didn't kill Joseph, their actions were very wrong, and they know it. The wrong they have done haunts them to the end of the story. We see, as we go on in the story, the brothers' consciences looking back, giving judgment against the wrong they had done.

Years later a famine in Canaan forces the ten brothers to go down to Egypt to buy food. Unknown to them, Joseph has become ruler of Egypt under the Pharaoh and is in charge of the food supplies. When Joseph recognizes his brothers, he arrests them on a charge of espionage. He says he will keep one of them hostage while the others go back to fetch their youngest brother (Joseph's only full brother, Benjamin). They are horrified and know that their father will not want to risk Benjamin's life after what happened to Joseph.

After this turn of events,

> They said to one another, 'Surely we are being punished because of our brother. We saw how distressed he was when he pleaded with us for his life, but we would not listen; that's why this distress has come on us.'

At which point Reuben says, 'Didn't I tell you not to sin against the boy? But you wouldn't listen! Now we must give an accounting for his blood' (Genesis 42:21–22).

All those years their guilty consciences have haunted them. Day after day, night after night, month after month, perhaps in dreams or nightmares, they have heard the distressed cries of Joseph as they threw him down the well and then as they sold him into slavery. Their consciences made sure they could never forget. They knew they were guilty and deserved to be punished.

The conscience of guilt uncovered

And then it happens again. The ten go and fetch Benjamin. When they come to leave, Joseph fills each man's sack full of food, puts back the money they paid, and puts his own precious silver cup in Benjamin's sack, so that it's as if the brothers have stolen both the money and the cup. After they leave, he sends after them, catches them, accuses them of stealing his cup and brings them back on trial.

When the sacks are opened, and the cup is found in Benjamin's sack, Judah says, 'God has uncovered your servants' guilt' (Genesis 44:16). But what guilt? They were not guilty of stealing the cup; Joseph had planted it on them! No, the guilt that God has uncovered is the guilt of selling Joseph into slavery and then lying to their father. All those years this guilt was like a time bomb waiting to explode.

Anticipated terror

When finally Joseph tells them who he is, we read, 'Joseph said to his brothers, "I am Joseph! Is my father still living?" But his brothers were not able to answer him, because they were terrified at his presence' (Genesis 45:3).

No wonder they were terrified: they stood before the man who had the power of life and death over them and they knew they were guilty. Their terror was not that of a guilty conscience. But it was the terror that a guilty conscience anticipates. All the pangs of conscience they had experienced over the preceding years were the warm-up to the terror they now experienced.

Still guilty even at the end

Finally, even at the very end of the story, when their father Jacob dies, the brothers say to one another, 'What if Joseph holds a grudge against us and pays us back for all the wrongs we did to him?' (Genesis 50:15).

A guilty conscience casts a long shadow.

A guilty conscience casts a long shadow. In his lively retelling of the Joseph story, Liam Goligher quotes an old writer who described conscience like this:

> Conscience 'is God's officer and vicegerent in man; set by him to be, as it were, thy angel, keeper, monitor, remembrance, king, prophet, examiner, judge – yea, thy lower heaven. If thou slightest it, it will be an adversary, informer, accuser, witness, judge, jailer, tormentor, a worm, rack, dungeon, unto thee – yea, thy upper hell.'[1]

As we think about our guilty consciences and what a guilty conscience does to us, here are nine important things to consider.

What a guilty conscience does

It never forgets

> Years ago, Kevin had lied in order to avoid a fine from a speed camera. He couldn't risk getting any more points on his licence. So he had told the police that the car was being driven by his friend Bonnie, and then he had paid the fine for her.
>
> It seemed such a trivial thing. And, he reasoned, he had paid the fine for her, so what was the problem? It hadn't mattered to her to get a few points on her licence and they had long since expired. No one else knew. And yet somehow Kevin couldn't forget telling that lie.

Conscience works through our memories. We have seen this with Joseph's brothers. It has been said that conscience keeps a diary. Our offence may be something we did years and years ago and erased from all our written and digital records. The electronic histories have been cleared. There is no document, no YouTube clip, no Internet trail of what we did or said. Perhaps no one else living knows or remembers what we did or failed to do. Maybe we ourselves are convinced that we have moved on in life. And yet it is part of our history, and we cannot manage to forget it. A guilty conscience never forgets; it is like an intestinal worm gnawing away inside us, unless it can somehow be cleansed (the wonderful subject of chapter 7).

It makes me want to hide

> Sarah was being interviewed for a job as a youth worker in her local church. The minister asked her, 'Is there any secret in your past that would bring dishonour to Jesus Christ if it came out into the open now?'

Sarah gulped. Yes, there was one. You and I don't need to know what it was, but Sarah carried it around with her in her heart. And the last thing she wanted was for it to be brought out into the open. So she said, 'No', gulped quietly and felt even worse than ever.

Secrecy is our natural response to a guilty conscience. Genesis 3 records Adam and Eve hiding from God in the garden. Of course they hid. The last thing a guilty conscience wants is to come out into the open and be exposed. It's no different for us. The last thing we want is for the full record of our failure to be projected onto the screen for all to see. We are like spiders scuttling away when the lights are turned on. As John's gospel puts it, 'Everyone who does evil hates the light, and will not come into the light for fear that their deeds will be exposed' (John 3:20). Joseph's brothers were horrified when God 'uncovered' their guilt.

One of the most terrifying examples of a hidden guilt being exposed is the Bible story of Achan in Joshua 7. I remember a speaker retelling the story in a way that made my hair stand on end, as he helped us imagine the feeling of mounting terror in Achan's heart as the lots were drawn and the arrow finally pointed not just at his tribe, not just at his clan within his tribe, not just at his family, but at Achan himself. A guilty conscience terrifies us with the fear of being found out.

It isolates me

Pete went out drinking with a group of friends. They drank too much, and it just happened to be the night on which gangs of rioters were setting fire to shops in the city. Pete and his friends would not normally have joined in, but under the influence of too many drinks they did, and looted an electrical goods store.

They were not caught. The police had more than enough to do catching the other looters.

When Pete went, as usual, to his church youth club the following weekend, he found himself feeling and acting curiously withdrawn. The others seemed so relaxed and cheerful. But although he was usually a cheerful extrovert, he suddenly felt alone.

Because our natural response to a guilty conscience is to want to hide, there will be an inbuilt tendency to loneliness. And it is interesting that when Joseph sends his brothers back to Canaan to fetch their father Jacob, he says to them, 'Don't quarrel on the way!' (Genesis 45:24). Joseph knows that guilty consciences drive people apart.

Although some evil promotes itself as a happy corporate act, the wild doings of a gang or the fun and games of a happy group of friends all joining in, the reality is that each will take away his or her own guilty conscience and will want to hide. A guilty conscience always reduces human community and isolates individuals. It foreshadows the terrible and total absence of friendship in hell.

It makes me fearful and anxious

While away on vacation, Jeff heard the news that his company was being audited by the IRS, who had gone into his office and confiscated both paper and digital media. He texted colleagues, who didn't seem too worried about this. But Jeff was scared stiff. There were things in his records that he really, really did not want the IRS to find. Quite suddenly this outwardly confident entrepreneur became a bundle of fears and nerves.

Although Joseph's brothers are capable of extremely violent behaviour, and no doubt of considerable bravado, a guilty conscience reduces them to very frightened men. William Fenner wrote that conscience 'is a powerful preacher; it exhorteth, urgeth, provoketh; yea, the most powerful preacher that can be; it will cause the stoutest and stubbornest heart under heaven to quake now and then.'[2] As Hamlet says, 'Conscience does make cowards of us all.'[3]

This is true. There is nothing that drains away a person's courage so quickly as a guilty conscience. We saw how scared Joseph's brothers were. We see this elsewhere in the Bible too. Early in his life, Moses saw an Egyptian beating a Hebrew, one of his own people. 'Looking this way and that and seeing no one, he killed the Egyptian and hid him in the sand' (Exodus 2:11–12). His motive was good, to protect the weak, but it was still murder, and he knew it. So when the next day he tried to sort out a fight between two of the Hebrews, and one of them asked him, 'Are you thinking of killing me as you killed the Egyptian?' Moses was very frightened and thought, 'What I did must have become known' (verses 13–14). Carrying around a guilty conscience, he also carried around the fear that what he had done would become known. It is the same with us. A guilty secret is a terrible burden to carry. At any time we may be exposed.

One of the paradoxes of conscience is that this fear can be triggered by the exposure of someone else's wrongdoing and not just by our own. When the people of Israel were travelling through the wilderness after the exodus from Egypt, there was a very serious incident of treason. The leadership of Moses was challenged by over 250 senior leaders (Numbers 16:1–3). It was what we would call an attempted coup. After being warned, the coup leaders are dramatically killed in some kind of earthquake, swallowed alive by the ground splitting apart (verse 31). As soon as this had happened, 'all the Israelites around them fled, shouting, "The earth is going to swallow us too!"' (verses 31–34). Although when Moses gave warning they had apparently distanced themselves from the coup leaders, their consciences told them that in their hearts raged the same rebellion. The punishment of the leaders aroused their own guilty consciences.

Something similar happens in the New Testament in the early days of the church. Ananias and Sapphira conspired deliberately and knowingly to lie so that people would think they had been more generous than in fact they had been (Acts 5:1–11). When the apostle Peter exposes their deceit, both of them in turn drop down dead. The fallout from this awful punishment was that 'great fear' came upon all sorts of other people (verse 11). Why were they frightened? No doubt some of that fear was from guilty consciences. They knew that they too deserved the punishment that had fallen on Ananias and Sapphira.

The Bible says that behind this fear lies a right fear of the judgment of God. Joseph's brothers realized that God had uncovered their guilt, and God was punishing them for it.

It is a heavy and painful burden

Calvin had a problem with alcohol. He wouldn't admit it to others but he knew it had the marks of an addiction. He couldn't help noticing that when he reached for the second drink, and the third, and the fourth, his pulse began to beat faster and he felt a sensation almost like physical pain. The conflict between what he knew would be right (to put the bottle away), and what he was hell-bent on doing, was tearing him apart.

Both the prospect of doing something wrong and the memory of having done something wrong cause us pain. One of the most vivid ways the Old Testament speaks of a guilty conscience is by the expression 'his heart smote him'; it is almost the language of having a heart attack. Twice when King David did something he knew to be wrong, we are told that 'his heart smote him'; the NIV translates this by saying he was 'conscience-stricken' (1 Samuel 24:5; 2 Samuel 24:10). It *hurt*.

The Bible is not the only place to tell us that a guilty conscience is painful. The Roman writer Plutarch says it is

> like an ulcer in the flesh. It implants in the soul a remorse which never ceases to wound and goad it. Any other pain can be reasoned away, but this remorse is inflicted by reason, on the soul which is so racked with shame, and self-chastised. For just as those overcome with shivering-fits, or burning with fever, suffer worse and are in greater distress than those who suffer the equivalent, but external, heat or cold, so the pains which come as it were from without . . . are more easy to bear. But the cry, 'None other is to blame for this but I myself' coming from within upon the wicked man's own sins, makes his sufferings yet harder to bear.[4]

The great seventeenth-century Christian theologian John Owen says that a guilty conscience makes 'an uproar in the soul' and gives it 'no rest or quiet until the soul be redeemed'.[5]

The plot of Ian McEwan's novel *Atonement* is driven by a guilty conscience. A deeply guilty person longs to find some means of making atonement. That this person does not find any real atonement is one of the tragedies of the story. It is both haunting and frightening.

There is a proverb that says, 'A happy heart makes the face cheerful, but heartache crushes the spirit' (Proverbs 15:13). A guilty conscience makes the heart ache. The hearts of Joseph's brothers ached with the guilt of what they had done. How often they must have wished they could rewind history and start all over again. But they couldn't.

In 1 Samuel 25 there is a terrible story of male stupidity and a wonderful story of female wisdom. Abigail (the lovely wise woman) is married to Nabal (whose name means 'fool' in Hebrew, which accurately sums up his nature). For some time David and his men have acted as informal protectors of Nabal's farm and property. When David asks for some hospitality in return, Nabal foolishly insults them. So much so that David sets out to teach Nabal a lesson with the sword. He is about to massacre them all, he is so angry.

Abigail, guessing that this is what will happen, wisely intercepts David with a present. She dissuades him from going on by saying to him that if he turns back, then when he becomes king he 'will not have on his conscience the staggering burden of needless bloodshed or of having avenged himself' (1 Samuel 25:31). She knows that if David repays the insult with an atrocity, he will carry around with him the 'staggering burden' of a guilty conscience. It is a wise appeal and one that David heeds. Indeed, he so appreciates a wise woman who appeals to his conscience that when Nabal dies of a heart attack, David marries her! It is a happy man whose wife will gently appeal to his conscience to head him off from doing evil like this.

It makes me angry and resentful

That morning around the office water cooler, Mike had badmouthed his boss unfairly. An hour or so later his boss, a kind and friendly woman, greeted him warmly and commended him on some work he had done. Mike grunted grumpily and was borderline rude in his response. He couldn't work out for the life of him why he had reacted like that, but somehow her kindness riled him after what he had said about her.

A guilty conscience is an inconsistency of the soul. It tears us apart and makes us hit out with a resentful anger at everyone and anyone. The strange and terrible story of Cain and his brother Abel (Genesis 4) begins with Cain and Abel each offering sacrifices to God. For some reason that is not spelled out in Genesis, God accepts Abel's offering but not Cain's (verses 4–5). The letter to the Hebrews tells us that it was because Abel's offering sprang from his trust in God, whereas Cain's did not (Hebrews 11:4). I suspect Cain wanted to make a deal with God:

'I scratch your back (by giving you something you want) and then you scratch mine (by giving me something I want).'

Whatever the reason, Cain had a guilty conscience, and his response was to get angry: 'So Cain was very angry, and his face was downcast' (verse 5).

I know in my experience that when I have done something I know to be wrong, I get irritable. I want someone else to blame (usually my wife, since she tends to be nearest). And so a guilty conscience sets us on a downward spiral. In the Cain and Abel story, the next thing God does is warn Cain that 'sin is crouching at your door' (verse 7). It is a vivid expression; we are to imagine sin like a wild animal crouching, ready to pounce. Cain is eaten up by anger. He is angry with himself, looking for any outlet for his anger and wanting to blame others for his plight. But the sad fact is that it is entirely his fault.

It makes me restless

Megan knew that for the past few years since college she had been living for herself. She had been pretty successful so far, with a smart apartment, a well-paying job and an enviable lifestyle. She hadn't done anything scandalously wrong, although from time to time she had been economical with the truth at work and pretty selfish when making excuses about why she hadn't helped a sick relative. But she knew in her heart that the whole aim of her life was, and had been, self-centred.

Although Megan had been a happy-go-lucky, carefree young woman, the longer she went on living like this, the more she began to feel a strange background residue of anxiety in her soul. She found it harder to relax, and she just couldn't work out why.

After he murders his brother Abel, Cain is told he will be 'a restless wanderer on the earth' (verse 12). For the remainder of his life, he is a troubled man. He cannot settle in his heart and soul.

When a man or woman with a guilty conscience is faced afresh with the consequences of their actions, they hate it. King Ahab was one of the worst of the Old Testament kings (and there was hot competition). When the prophet Elijah met him, he famously addressed Elijah as 'you troubler of Israel' and 'my enemy' (1 Kings 18:17; 21:20). He too was a restless man. A word of truth unsettled him. A guilty conscience makes it hard for us to settle, to find peace in our hearts and minds, to be, as we say, 'comfortable in our own skin'.

It makes us look for religious solutions

The American pornography millionaire Rob Black was interviewed by *The Guardian*. The interviewer wrote that on Black's neck, 'Alongside a tiny silver medallion depicting the Virgin Mary is something that looks like one of those clothing labels that give optimum washing temperatures. It turns out to be a piece of parchment, bearing the hand-written legend: "Whoever dies wearing this scapular shell shall not suffer eternal fire." Expecting a gag, I ask what this means. For once, Black's triumphant voice is flat and without scorn. "If I die wearing this," he says calmly and very rationally, "I won't burn in hell."'[6]

Latoya enjoyed her high-powered and well-paying job as a management consultant. She had secured the job on the strength of her outstanding PhD on the psychological factors involved with business leadership. What no one knew was that one critical part of that PhD had been plagiarized from an obscure paper published in another part of the world.

The examiners had not detected this, and it seemed unlikely anyone ever would. Latoya's job and reputation were in no danger. Or so she repeatedly told herself. But Latoya could not forget what she had done. She knew it was wrong, and it made her feel bad inside. When friends congratulated her on getting this top job, rather than feeling pleased and affirmed, she felt sour and sick. Although she wanted to come clean and lance the boil, she didn't dare do it. So she hugged her guilty secret to her heart and began to have trouble sleeping and to become an uncharacteristically anxious person.

And then she found religion. In her case it was a sort of Christianity, but really it might have been any other religion. Greatly to her parents' and friends' surprise, she began to attend Holy Communion on Sundays and midweek, to read her Bible and say her prayers almost obsessively. No one knew why. But it didn't seem to do her any good. Still she couldn't sleep. Still she was riddled with nameless fears.

A guilty conscience is a terrible thing. We will see in chapter 6 that one strategy to reduce the pain is to harden ourselves. But another is to seek solace in religion, in the hope that doing something religious can persuade God to overlook our guilt. The Bible describes God as 'he who weighs the heart'. For example, in the book of Proverbs we read,

> Rescue those being led away to death;
> > hold back those staggering towards slaughter.
> If you say, 'But we knew nothing about this,'
> > does not he who weighs the heart perceive it?
> (Proverbs 24:11–12)

The implication of the proverb is that the hearers knew of some atrocity. While it is hard not to think of the Holocaust as an extreme example, there may be other atrocities closer to home, such as how our society treats older people. The point of the proverb is that the excuse that we didn't know will not hold water before God, 'who weighs the heart'. He knows that I knew. My conscience tells me that he knows that I knew.

This description of God as the one who 'weighs the heart' parallels something from the Egyptian *Book of the Dead*. In 2010, the British Museum in London put on a stunning exhibition of papyrus scrolls with spells on them to help dead people get right through to the afterlife. The most riveting scene is the judgment, in which the person's heart is weighed on a pair of scales against the principle of right and wrong (what the Egyptians called *Ma'at*), which is represented by a feather, to make the point that the person was bound to fail. I suppose their guilty conscience told them they would never match up to their own standards.

So the purpose of the spells was to fool the god doing the weighing into thinking we had passed the test. It was a desire to use a religious practice to deal with a guilty conscience. But the Bible teaches us that no spell will fool the true God 'who weighs the heart'.

It can lead finally to despair

Some (though of course not all) suicides are the ultimate despair of a guilty conscience. The Jewish philosopher Philo wrote that if conscience 'cannot prevail' (that is, to make someone change their life),

> it gives not peace, but makes war. Never does it depart by day nor by night, but it stabs as with a goad, and inflicts wounds that know no healing, until it snap the thread of that soul's pitiful and accursed life.[7]

We see a contemporary fictional example of the pain of a guilty conscience in Bernhard Schlink's book *The Reader*. In this novel a guilty conscience drives someone to despair many years later.

In the book of Deuteronomy, Moses warns the people of Israel of the consequences of being unfaithful to God, the only source of blessing and life (chapter 28). If you turn away from him, warns Moses, you must expect terrible results. Near the end of the chapter he says,

> Among those nations [that is, the nations of Israel's exile] you will find no repose, no resting place for the sole of your foot. There the LORD will give you an anxious mind, eyes weary with longing, and a despairing heart. You will live in constant suspense, filled with dread both night and day, never sure of your life (Deuteronomy 28:65–66).

This is the end result of a guilty conscience. As Jeremiah put it hundreds of years later, at the time of the exile to Babylon,

> Your own conduct and actions
>   have brought this upon you.
> This is your punishment.
>   How bitter it is!
>   How it pierces to the heart!
> (Jeremiah 4:18)

How terrible it is to know that this is my fault, that I can blame no one else, and that I must now live with the consequences of my 'own conduct and actions'.

Conscience: God's courtroom

Someone has said that conscience is like God's courtroom set up in the human heart. It contains five things that we find in a courtroom.[8]

First, it keeps records, just as the clerk of the court will write things down accurately. Conscience keeps diaries; it writes down everything we have ever said, seen and done, and also the things we have not said or done that we ought to have done. It is all recorded and cannot be erased.

Second, conscience acts as a witness. There is such a thing as 'the testimony of our conscience'. Our conscience speaks up, either for or against us, in any given instance.

Third, conscience functions like a prosecuting counsel, cross-examining us and exposing our guilt. Conscience can accuse (Romans 2:15).

Fourth, conscience acts as a judge inside us. It passes judgment on us, saying, 'That was right. That was wrong.'

Fifth and finally, conscience is like an executioner or agent of punishment, carrying out the punishment decreed by the judge. It does this in a partial way. If conscience tells us we deserve to die, it does not kill us immediately (or at least not usually). But it gives us, before our death, 'a flash of hell' in the present. Just as David's heart 'smote him' (1 Samuel 24:5), so our consciences give us grief, which is an anticipation of the punishment to come.

A guilty conscience is a terrible thing. All of us know what it is. There are things in my life, as there will be in yours, of which I am deeply ashamed. Whether they be things I have done or failed to do, things I have said or failed to say, things I have read, watched and enjoyed, or things I have thought, my conscience sits, as it were, on my shoulder and says, 'That was wrong. That was wicked. That was impure. That was uncaring. That was lazy. That was neglectful. That was untruthful. That was greedy. And it was your fault. You cannot blame anyone else.' And it hurts, and I really hate it.

It was a guilty conscience that drove Judas Iscariot to suicide. If a way exists that will really make a guilty conscience clean, it is of the utmost importance that we find it. That is the wonderful subject of chapter 7. But before we get there, we need to pause and ask ourselves what we must learn from the experience of a guilty conscience. It is a symptom of something—but of what?

Questions for personal study or discussion

Think honestly about each of the nine characteristics of a guilty conscience.

1. Is there anything in your past that still makes you feel guilty and that you want to hide? Why can't you forget it?

2. Have you ever felt isolated or withdrawn because of feeling guilty?

3. Have you ever been frightened because of past guilt?

4. Do you feel the pain of a guilty conscience? Is your conscience driving you close to despair?

5. Is guilt making you angry or resentful?

6. Have you experienced an unresolved guilt that makes you restless?

7. Do you try to find religious ways of dealing with a guilty conscience?

Notes

1. Andrew Fuller, quoted in Liam Goligher, *Joseph* (Christian Focus, 2008), p. 123.
2. William Fenner, *A Treatise of Conscience* (1651), quoted in David Watson, *Know Yourself* (IVP, 1964), p. 6.
3. Shakespeare, *Hamlet*, Act 3, Scene i.
4. Quoted in C. A. Pierce, *Conscience in the New Testament* (SCM, 1955), p. 47.
5. John Owen, *The Nature and Power of Indwelling Sin* in *Works* (Richard Baynes, 1826), vol. XIII, p. 97.
6. Reported in *Church Times*, 28 November 1997, p. 21.
7. Quoted in Pierce, *Conscience*, p. 46.
8. Richard Sibbes, quoted in J. I. Packer, *Among God's Giants: The Puritan Vision of the Christian Life* (Kingsway, 1991), p. 145.

5

THE AWAKENED CONSCIENCE

When in the paths of sin we move
and so the living God forsake,
our conscience by your word reprove,
convince and bring the wanderers back,
deep wounding by your Spirit's sword,
and then by pardoning grace restored.[1]

Gavin was about to go home from church at the end of the third week of the enquirers' course. In many ways he was loving it. He listened with rapt attention to the Bible being taught. He asked thoughtful and genuine questions. He looked forward to the course from week to week and felt that something very big and very wonderful was happening in his life.

But just before he left he asked if he could have a word with the course leader. 'There's one thing that puzzles and troubles me,' he said. 'Before I started hearing the Bible being taught, my life was bumbling along not too badly. I did sometimes feel a bit bad about gossiping about people behind their backs or about ruthlessly pushing my career forward with little respect for others. But not very bad, and not for long, to be honest. But now I am beginning to feel much worse about that sort of gossip and ruthlessness, painfully worse. Sometimes at night I get really anxious and troubled about the kind of person I am and the fact that I join in and enjoy tearing others down. Can you explain why I feel so much worse now? You tell me Christianity is good news. So why should hearing it make me feel so terrible?'

A challenged conscience faces us with a choice

In the last chapter we saw how Abigail appealed to David's conscience in her attempt to dissuade him from massacring her family and ransacking her farm, and how her attempt was successful (1 Samuel 25). But it might not have been. When someone appeals to my conscience (whether or not they use 'conscience' language) to dissuade me from doing something, or to ask me to apologize and turn away from some past behaviour, I am faced with a choice. It is never pleasant to hear that kind of appeal, for it always contains an element of rebuke, stirring up in me the bad feelings of a guilty conscience. It is not a happy experience and it hurts to be made aware that I have done something wrong or that I was set on doing something wrong. But it also confronts me with a choice: how am I going to respond? (We will continue to think about this in the next two chapters.)

The apostle Paul had to give that kind of rebuke to the young church in Corinth, appealing to their consciences to change their behaviour. He had a troubled relationship with this lively but unruly church. Sometime between his first (1 Corinthians) and second letter (2 Corinthians) he seems to have written them another letter. That letter caused them pain, almost certainly because it contained a rebuke for some wrong behaviour in the church. But listen to how he reflects on this pain:

Even if I caused you sorrow by my letter, I do not regret it. Though I did regret it – I see that my letter hurt you, but only for a little while – yet now I am happy, not because you were made sorry, but because your sorrow led you to repentance. For you became sorrowful as God intended and so were not harmed in any way by us. Godly sorrow brings repentance that leads to salvation and leaves no regret, but worldly sorrow brings death (2 Corinthians 7:8–10).

Paul talks here about two kinds of sorrow: godly sorrow and worldly sorrow. He doesn't say much about worldly sorrow here, because – thank God – they didn't show it. He just says it 'brings death'.

Godly sorrow responds to a guilty conscience with repentance

Audrey was in her seventies. She loved it when her grandson Sam came to visit. But last time Sam came around, he said something that really upset her. With the tactless honesty of an eight-year-old, Sam blurted out, 'Nan, I wish you didn't complain so much. You're always moaning about your health or your neighbours or something.' Of course Sam's mom had told him off for speaking to his granny like that, and the conversation had moved on.

But Audrey felt bad. Sam was right. She rationalized it by saying that things were really tough for her. She was widowed, lonely and housebound. Her body was weak and hurt a lot. Her neighbours weren't very considerate. But, she realized, she had become self-absorbed and self-pitying. She needed to change. Quietly Audrey prayed and asked her heavenly Father to make her more thankful day by day for all his kindness and mercies.

Audrey didn't like what her grandson had said. It caused her sorrow. But it was a godly sorrow. By contrast with the worldly sorrow that leads to death, and is therefore permanent and unending, Paul says that godly sorrow is temporary ('only for a little while'). By contrast with worldly sorrow that leads to no change of life, this godly sorrow 'led you to repentance'. It is a sorrow 'as God intended', the kind of grief God wants us to have in response to a guilty conscience. By contrast with worldly sorrow that leads to death, and therefore harms us irreparably, this sorrow leaves no trace of regret afterwards, no sour taste in the mouth, because it is a sorrow that 'leads to salvation'. Paradoxically, this is therefore a good sorrow in every way.

I am going to call this sorrow the awakening of the conscience. When a friend of mine was asked what had happened when he came to Christ, he said, 'My conscience was awakened.' He explained to me that of course he had always known what it was to feel bad about doing or saying bad things. But when he came to faith in Christ his conscience was awakened, so that he learned what his guilty conscience meant and responded to it with heart repentance.

When Ezra read the covenant law of God to the returned exiles in Jerusalem,[2] their response was to mourn and weep in repentance for the sin of which they were convicted. They were told not to mourn and weep (Nehemiah 8:9), not because their response had been inappropriate, but precisely because it had been appropriate. The paradox is that if they *hadn't* wept, they would have been told they ought to weep! But when they were deeply convicted of their sin, their consciences were awakened and they wept; then they were in a fit state to receive gospel comfort. It is the same with us today.

Godly sorrow is a gracious work of the Spirit of God

When our oldest son was a boy, he was taken to the hospital with what seemed like most of the gravel of our front driveway in the skin of his knee and leg. He had fallen at high speed off his BMX. As the doctor prepared to clean out the wound, I imagine he said, with that characteristic understatement of doctors, 'This may hurt a bit.' I'm sure it did hurt, quite a lot. But, as the doctor no doubt explained, the alternatives were far worse – things like blood poisoning, tetanus, gangrene, or even having his leg amputated! It was worth the smaller pain to save the bigger pain later.

In the same way, the pain of a guilty conscience is necessary if the disease of the heart is to be healed. By nature, we respond to a guilty conscience with worldly sorrow. We are sorry for the nasty *consequences* of bad things we have done, but not really deeply sorry for the things themselves. Our sorrow hurts, but it is superficial. It is like the pain of the injury rather than the pain of the doctor treating the injury.

Jesus said that the Spirit of God would bring conviction to the world, and that would begin with conviction of sin (John 16:8–9). Conviction comes when I am inwardly convinced, when I become conscious, aware in my awakened conscience, about my sin. This conviction comes from the Spirit of God. The Spirit of God is not the same as my conscience, for the Spirit of God is God, the third person of the Trinity, and my conscience is just a part of me. But he uses my conscience to bring conviction to my heart, especially conviction of my sinfulness.

And so, paradoxically, when the Spirit of God gets to work in our lives to begin God's rescue, he starts by making our guilty conscience hurt more, abominably more, than it had ever done before. He takes the wound and opens it up. He does this in order to cleanse and heal. But it certainly hurts! When my conscience is awakened, God himself is at work to wake up my drugged and sleepy conscience. He is going to use my wide-awake and alert conscience to turn me around from heading full-speed towards death. The experience will hurt horribly to start with, but only for a little while.

An Old Testament example of godly sorrow
There is a vivid example of this godly sorrow in the Old Testament, a few years before the people of Israel were exiled

to Babylon. The young king Josiah started a program of restoration work on the neglected Jerusalem temple (2 Kings 22). During the building work, the high priest stumbled on 'the Book of the Law' (presumably part of the law of Moses). It is a sign of how bad things had got in Judah that their equivalent to the Bible had effectively been lost. When they blew the dust off it, they took it to King Josiah and read it to him. It must have made for uncomfortable listening, since it contained details of the covenant or agreement between God and his people. This covenant specified that if the people were faithful and trusted God with loving obedience, then he would bless them wonderfully. But if they were unfaithful, unbelieving and disobedient, then they would bring upon themselves terrible curses. It was a reading that stirred up the painful experience of a guilty conscience.

How did the king respond? Wonderfully, with what Paul would call 'godly sorrow'. He tore his robes as a sign of penitence. He understood that God was rightly very angry with his people. He humbled himself before God. He was very sorry when sin was exposed, yet his sorrow was a godly sorrow that led to repentance.

A vivid Old Testament example of an awakened conscience

Darren is a respectable Christian and CEO of a multinational company. He is also a lay preacher. But he develops an infatuation with Natasha, a junior colleague who is a married woman. Natasha's husband also works for the company and is overseas for some months. So this senior man uses his seniority and power to seduce Natasha, to persuade or compel her to sleep with him.

And then he learns to his horror that he has made her pregnant. He is very sorry. Not sorry that he has slept with her.

But sorry that he may be found out and his respectability will be called into question and his reputation ruined. So what does he do? He is the CEO, a very powerful man. He finds a pretext to get Natasha's husband home quickly, so that when the pregnancy becomes known everyone will assume the husband is the father of the child. But something goes wrong and the husband doesn't manage to get home as planned.

Darren is desperate to protect his reputation. And so, even more shockingly, he hires a contract killer to murder the husband and make it appear an accident. The husband is killed. Darren quickly marries Natasha. And it's all covered up. He gets ready to preach at a church the next Sunday. Never mind that he has abused his power repeatedly, committed adultery, lied, deceived and been instrumental in murder. Nobody knows or suspects.

If you are a Bible reader, you will recognize that I have taken the terrible story of David and Bathsheba from 2 Samuel 11 and 12 and set its essential plotline in a contemporary cultural context. It is an extreme story. Few if any of us can match all its terrible ingredients in our pasts. But I think that may be the point. If, as the conclusion to this story shows us, confession and forgiveness are possible for such a catalogue of wickedness, then it shows you and me how confession and forgiveness are possible for whatever there may be in your past or mine.

David thought he had covered up well, but the prophet Nathan confronted him (2 Samuel 12). He showed him that God knew about it and it could not be covered up. He stirred up David's guilty conscience. And, just as when Abigail appealed to his conscience (1 Samuel 25), again David had a choice. David's response is found in Psalm 51, which is headed, 'A psalm of David. When the prophet Nathan came to him after David had committed adultery with Bathsheba'. The psalm shows how a man with an awakened conscience responds to guilt.

If Psalm 51 features in popular culture at all, it tends to be as a miserable parody of Christianity. In the film of the book *Chocolat*, the weak Roman Catholic priest reads from Psalm 51 as the spokesman for the sad, repressed figure of the mayor. The psalm stands for repressed emotions, the denial of joy and a deeply unattractive self-righteous religion. Indeed, the film pits this against an attractively portrayed hedonism, which seems to be the only alternative. And yet, properly understood, Psalm 51 speaks with the voice of an awakened conscience, which is the only road to the joy of a cleansed conscience. The hedonism portrayed as so attractive is in reality not attractive at all, or at least not in the end, because it leads to regret rather than thanksgiving and to selfishness rather than care for others.

The Psalm begins with a cry for mercy and cleansing (verses 1–2), a cry that is drawn out of David by the pain of a guilty conscience (verse 3): 'For I know my transgressions, and my sin is always before me.'

David says, 'I know my transgressions'; I have become deeply self-aware of them, conscious of them, I have a wide-awake conscience about them, and therefore I am going to 'know' them in the sense of 'acknowledging' them, coming clean about them. And he says that his sin 'is always before me'. Someone has described this as a 'shameful, waking nightmare'. Every morning David wakes and thinks, 'What have I done?' Every time he sees the marks of pregnancy on Bathsheba he asks himself, 'What have I done?' Every day he walks past the graveyard where Uriah is buried he cries out in inner anguish, 'What have I done?' He cannot put his sin behind him; it is always there, staring him in the face. Like Lady Macbeth faced with the bloody evidence of murder, David wants to cry out, 'Here's the smell of blood still: all the perfumes of Arabia will not sweeten this little hand'.[3] I spoke recently to a man who had become a Christian in mid-life, after which he looked back at all the people he had ever hurt and just wept and wept and wept. This was David's experience too:

What have I done? How could I have done that? I wish I could rewind the clock; but I can't.

But the psalm does not end there. David goes on to show that by the Spirit of God he has learned at least three terrible but necessary truths about himself through the experience of a guilty conscience. We too can learn about the direction, the origin and the depth of our sinfulness.

Marks of an awakened conscience

The direction of sin

David says – and this is very surprising – 'Against you, you only, have I sinned and done what is evil in your sight' (verse 4). It seems obvious that David has sinned against other people. He has wronged Uriah horribly by committing adultery with his wife and then arranging for him to be killed. He has wronged Bathsheba by using his power to seduce or compel her to sleep with him. He has wronged Joab, his army commander, by ordering him to be complicit in the murder of Uriah. How can he say to God, 'Against you, you *only*, have I sinned'?

I do not think David wants for one moment to minimize the wrongs he has done to Uriah, Bathsheba, Joab, or anyone else. But what David has grasped is this: at its deepest level, all the terrible things he has done are directed against God. At root, the adultery, the deceit and the murder are not about the people he has hurt, but about a mindset that thinks it can live in God's world without worshipping and honouring him. Nathan the prophet has said to him, 'you have shown utter contempt for the LORD' (2 Samuel 12:14), and David can see that this is true. His contempt for Uriah, his demeaning of Bathsheba and his thoughtlessness about Joab all have their root in an utter contempt for God. As Michael Wilcock puts it, David 'sees no longer before him the glamour of the woman he stole, nor even beside him the innocence of the man he killed, but behind him the judgment of the God he had turned his back on'.[4]

An awakened conscience grasps and admits that I do not basically love and honour God even though I sometimes mess up with people. On the contrary, it admits that by nature I am someone who has contempt for God, who does not honour God as God and does not bow down to him. The reason I get it wrong with people is that I do not love and honour God.

We may put this truth more generally by saying that social sin (wrong treatment of others) is theological in its root (contempt of God). Mistreating people is insulting God. As Proverbs puts it, 'whoever oppresses the poor shows contempt for their Maker' (Proverbs 14:31). Or, as John puts it in his first letter, if I mistreat people whom I can see, I cannot claim to love God, whom I cannot see (1 John 4:20). This is why, when God gets taken out of the equation, ethics becomes relativistic. It is just a question of comparing myself with other people, and I can always find other people who behave worse than I do, which makes me feel all right about my behaviour. The root of justice is God the judge. As James Mays says in his commentary on Psalm 51, without God the whole vocabulary of sin 'becomes meaningless and atrophies'.[5]

So the first mark of an awakened conscience is to learn from my guilty conscience that the root problem lies in my relationship with God.

The origin of sin

Beth has a sharp tongue. Last night when she came back from a party, she said something very cutting to her mom. She was sorry afterwards, when she saw how much she had hurt her mom. Later she was telling her friend Karen, and Karen asked, 'Why do you do it?' 'I only wish I knew,' said Beth. 'I love my mom lots, and basically I've always thought I was a kind and gentle person. And yet again and again and again I lash out at her, and at other people too. I just wish I knew why.'

David goes on to say, 'Surely [certainly] I was sinful at birth, sinful from the time my mother conceived me' (Psalm 51:5). He can see that he is not basically a good person who slips up from time to time. No, he says, my wrong actions are not isolated exceptions. They are the evidence that I myself am a guilty person. He admits, 'I was sinful', not just 'I happened to commit a sin'.

It is not enough just to admit that a particular action was wrong; I must admit that I myself am in the wrong before God. Facing the terrible judgment of exile, Jeremiah or one of his contemporaries wrote five eloquent Lamentations. In the first one, he says,

> See, LORD, how distressed I am!
>   I am in torment within,
> and in my heart I am disturbed,
>   for I have been most rebellious.
> (Lamentations 1:20)

It is not just that I have slipped carelessly into an isolated act of rebellion; no, it is I myself as a whole person who have been rebellious.

Jesus told the parable of the Pharisee and the tax collector to contrast this kind of admission with smug self-righteousness (Luke 18:9–14). He begins with the Pharisee, who is confident of his own righteousness, looks down on other people and thanks God that he is not as bad as they are. Self-righteousness masquerades as a clear conscience. It is the veneer of spiritual contentedness glued over the ugliness of human pride. It is the easy way to feel good about myself. The strategy is simple and popular. First, I should compare myself not to the holiness of God, but to the behaviour of others, taking care to choose those others carefully so that I look good by comparison. Then I can feel good about how much better I behave they do.

But then Jesus directs our attention to the despised and morally compromised tax collector, who prays, 'God, have mercy on me, a sinner'.

So it's not ' . . . on me, who have sinned' but ' . . . on me, a sinner'. The second mark of an awakened conscience is encapsulated in those words, 'me, a sinner'. This is echoed in the words of Richard III in Shakespeare's play of that name:

My conscience hath a thousand several tongues
And every tongue brings in a several tale,
And every tale condemns me for a villain.[6]

In a way, this admission was the great rediscovery of Martin Luther at the time of the Protestant Reformation in the early sixteenth century. Some of the medieval theologians had spoken of conscience as one aspect of practical reason. God gave us some general laws, and conscience is the moral reasoning which enables us to apply these to particular situations. It is all rather quiet, calm, rational and intellectual. Luther understood – and particularly from the Psalms – that, while this might be true, it did not go nearly far enough. An awakened conscience does much more than show me that a particular action was (or would be) wrong; it shows me that I myself, as a whole person, am under the just judgment of God.[7]

What is more, an awakened conscience shows me that my sinful nature goes right back to the very beginnings of my existence: 'Surely I was sinful at birth, sinful from the time my mother conceived me' (Psalm 51:5). David looks back to those two poles of his origin, his birth and his conception. If you want to sum up the beginnings of a person in a radical way, go right back to their birth and beyond that to the instant of their conception, before which they did not exist.

David is not saying that there was anything especially sinful about his particular conception, or that sex is intrinsically sinful, for within marriage it is good. No, he is saying that if you go right back to my birth, and even before that to my conception, you will find that I was a sinner. I am a sinner not just by the influences of the world and the devil upon me, not just by a dysfunctional childhood or the wicked influences of a godless society, but in my origins. From the moment my father's sperm fused with my mother's egg, from that instant right at the root and origin of my existence, I had a sinful nature. David is confessing his sinful nature. It's not just that I do sin, but that I am a sinner.

This is the tragedy and ambiguity of human existence. As I was writing this chapter, I received a joyful text from dear friends to say their baby son had been safely born. 'Hooray, hooray!' I texted back, sharing their joy. But I know them well enough to know that they will not forget that that sweet and beautiful baby (as I am sure he is) is another sinner, conceived by sinners and sinful in his origins, going right back to Adam and Eve. Beautiful and sweet and loved as he is, he is a sinner in need of a Saviour.

Alec Motyer has said,

> It is the child, indeed the embryo at the very split-second of conception, that carries the infection of sin. The sexual union of father and mother is itself pure and holy, yet it is the means of transmitting the reality of the fallen human nature to the next generation.[8]

This is sometimes called the doctrine of original sin, which means that our sinful nature goes right back to our origins in the first human man and woman. In his letter to the church in Rome, Paul says that 'sin entered the world through one man, and death through sin, and in this way death came to all people, because all sinned' (Romans 5:12).

Sin entered the world when Adam disobeyed God. And then the sinful nature has been transmitted by natural human procreation to every human being ever since, with only one exception. After Genesis 3 everything changes: 'There is no objective tempter in Genesis 4. It would seem that humankind no longer needed a talking serpent; the promptings are all inward, the acts are those that come "naturally" to the agents.'[9]

This is a very important truth. Article 9 of the 39 Articles of the Church of England puts it like this (the left-hand column is the original; the right-hand one is my explanatory paraphrase).

Original Sin standeth not in the following of *Adam* . . .	Original sin does not just mean we follow Adam's example.
but it is the fault and corruption of the Nature of every man, that naturally is ingendered of the offspring of *Adam*;	It means that our human nature is corrupted (for all who are conceived and born naturally, i.e. everyone except the Lord Jesus Christ).
whereby man is very far gone from original righteousness, and is of his own nature inclined to evil, so that the flesh lusteth always contrary to the spirit; and therefore in every person born into this world, it deserveth God's wrath and damnation.	This means we are a long way away from being naturally good. By nature we are inclined to evil and wanting to think, say and do bad things, and therefore deserve God's settled anger and punishment.
And this infection of nature doth remain, yea in them that are regenerated; whereby the lust of the flesh . . . is not subject to the Law of God.	Even born-again individuals (Christians) still have this original sinful nature.

To admit that I have a sinful nature means admitting that my wrong inclinations (the wrong things I desire, or for that matter the good things I do not delight in) are wrong, just as much as my wrong actions are. I am guilty for the corrupt nature that inclines me to sin even before I act out those inclinations.[10]

When the first human beings sinned, a blight spread through all humanity, like dry rot in the old timbers of a house. This is who I am, sinful and guilty from birth. Sin is something I cannot escape from, whatever decisions I take. We sometimes speak loosely of 'people of goodwill'. But no human being has a truly good will until that will is changed by Christ.

David is not saying, 'please wash my sin off me', as if there is a clean 'me' underneath. He is saying, 'wash *me*'. It is striking that in this psalm the distress of David does not come from being sick, or from being attacked or persecuted. His distress comes from within, as he sees the ugliness of his nature. This is the second mark of an awakened conscience. And it hurts.

The depth of sin

Barry had installed Covenant Eyes[11] on his laptop to keep himself from looking at pornography. The Covenant Eyes filter blocked any unsuitable websites. And if he ever overrode the filter, his accountability partners Rick and Tom were notified. It was a good thing to do, and Barry was glad he had put it in place. But what troubled him was that he still found himself with lustful desires in his heart. Even though he had done what he could to prevent himself from looking at pornography, he still *wanted* to. It was as if he had a split personality.

In Psalm 51, David's awareness (his consciousness or conscience) that he is sinful by nature, and that this goes right back to his origins, is matched by a sense that this nature is deep and not just superficial. It would be so nice to think that what David had done was like getting mud on your clothes during a wet winter walk, that he was basically a sound and healthy person who happened to get dirty. But his prayer shows that he knows this is not so. He prays not for a surface polish, but for deep inner cleansing. We see this especially in verse 10 where he prays for

God to 'Create in me a pure *heart* . . . and renew a steadfast [reliable] *spirit* within me'. The heart and the spirit here are two ways of speaking about me deep inside, at the deepest level of human personhood.

David needs a work of God's Holy Spirit to do something so deep and radical within him that he himself will be changed (verse 11). He needs to be given a new spirit that will be 'willing' (that is, willing to do God's will) (verse 12). He does not pray just for changed words or changed behaviour, but for a changed heart.

A friend helped me to understand this by using an illustration. Suppose I hold a glass of water and I shake it. Water spills out, and you ask me, 'Why did water spill out?' The instinctive answer is, 'Water came out because you shook it.' But there is another correct answer, which is, 'Water came out because water is what was inside the glass. If there hadn't been water in the glass in the first place, no water would ever have come out of the glass.' Sure, it *came out* because it was shaken. But *water* came out because *water* was inside.

So if we ask David, 'Why did you do what you did?', he might say, 'I did it because I was tempted, because of pressure. I was, as it were, shaken. My equilibrium was disturbed by outside influences, things that happened to me. I was weary. I looked out of the window and saw this beautiful woman, and one thing led to another. I was shaken.' That's what we instinctively say. 'I said that because I was stressed.' 'I did that because I was tired, or sick.' 'My upbringing has conditioned me to react that way.'

But David's deep answer is, 'I committed adultery because there is adultery in my heart'; 'I covered up because there is pride in my heart'; 'I murdered because love of self and hatred of others is in my heart'. The really shocking thing I have discovered, says David, is that what I did expressesed who I am. Evil came out of me because there is evil in me. What David did was not ultimately out of character, but a terrible revelation of the fallen character of his heart. David's awakened conscience acknowledges this hard truth in this psalm.

And it is true for us too. That cutting remark came out of me because there is pride in my heart. That defensive hostility showed itself in that meeting because there is a selfish insecurity in my heart. That misleading email that showed a colleague in a bad light came out of me because there is malice in my heart. The cover-up lie had its roots in a selfish regard for my reputation. The failure to give was because of a love of money. The laziness arose because the thought in my heart is that the world owes me a living. And so on. And therefore the proper response is deep. As the prophet Joel put it, 'Rend your heart and not your garments' (Joel 2:13). To tear one's clothes in Old Testament culture could be just a superficial thing, going through the culturally recognized symbols of mourning for sin. What is needed is a torn and broken heart, which is much more painful.

It's ugly, isn't it? And it goes very deep. It is deep in its direction, an alienation from God; deep in its origins, part of being in a fallen humanity; deep in its root, in my heart and my spirit. It is theological, original and spiritual.

But these three marks of an awakened conscience are signs that God is at work, and therefore signs of hope. They do not make the pain of conscience any the less; indeed, they make the pain more acute, for there is no easy get-out clause. With an awakened conscience we can blame no one else, we cannot minimize the seriousness of our guilt, and we should not harden ourselves against it. On the contrary, we feel the pain and terror of it to its full extent.

An awakened conscience is a painful sign of hope

An awakened conscience is both a wonderful and a terrible thing. It brings a sorrow that hurts abominably, and yet it leaves no regrets. It opens my eyes to the Godward direction of my sin, that the root of my problems is trying to live in God's world without honouring him. It opens my eyes to the personal origins of my sin: I am responsible for it, and yet I cannot escape its clutches and grasp without a Saviour. It opens my eyes to the depth of my sin, showing that the reason why nasty stuff comes out of me is because there is nasty stuff in my heart.

None of these responses is natural. The natural response to a guilty conscience is not to acknowledge God, not to admit original sin and not to face the fact of sin deep in the heart. (We will look at the natural responses in the next chapter.) But when these marks of an awakened conscience are present, we have grounds for hope that the Spirit of God is at work and that our sorrow will lead to salvation.

What does conscience have to do with real Christianity?

It was going to be an exciting evening service. Three people would tell the story of how they had recently become Christians.

Freddie went first: 'I had lost my job and was really worried that our house would be repossessed. But then I became a Christian, and the next week I got an even better-paying job. We've kept the house, repaid more of the mortgage and bought a really smart convertible car. Jesus is amazing!'

Stella spoke second: 'I used to suffer from depression and low self-esteem. It was a long and painful struggle. But then last month I became a Christian. My depression has lifted and I feel so much better about myself. Jesus is wonderful!'

Jeff came to the microphone and said, 'I was respectable, happily married, in a steady job, with no great dramas in my life. But the Bible taught me that I am guilty before God. I began to feel guilty, terribly guilty, for living in God's world without him. Thank God that Jesus died to pay the penalty for my guilt, and now I am his disciple.'

Which of these three stories do you think was the most exciting? The most moving? The most authentic? If we were playing 'Spot the real conversion', which would it be? All three stories may well be true and we can't know for sure which, if any, of these three have really become Christians in their hearts and forever. But which story do you think rings true with the sound of real Christianity?

The Christian gospel begins with the pain of an awakened conscience

Real Christianity awakens the conscience. Christianity tells people the truth, first of God's standards (his good law) and then of the gospel of the Lord Jesus, so that their consciences will be awakened, they will have a deep conscious sense of their need of forgiveness, and they will find rescue in Christ alone.

Jesus Christ may give an unemployed man a job, as happened to Freddie. But that is not the gospel, and God does not promise it. Jesus may make a depressed person feel better, as happened to Stella. But that is not the gospel, and God does not promise it. What he does promise is to forgive the sin of the sinner whose conscience is awakened so that they know and feel their sin and their need to be made clean. It is this to which Jeff testifies. This sounds like the real thing.

There is nothing automatic about this awakening. The gospel is 'veiled' to some (2 Corinthians 4:3). Some will experience a guilty conscience but not an awakened conscience. They will find ways of silencing their conscience so that it gradually troubles them less and less.

The only way into real Christianity is via a conscience awakened by the Holy Spirit. The usual instrument God uses to awaken conscience is his law. We have seen that you and I do not need the law of God to have some sense of right and wrong and therefore to have a good or bad conscience. We all have our own standards and we know the misery of being torn apart by knowing we have failed to keep our own standards. As James puts it in his New Testament letter, 'Anyone . . . [who] knows the good they ought to do and doesn't do it, it is sin for them' (James 4:17). If my conscience tells me I ought to do something and I fail to do it, I sin. I cannot even keep my own standards.

But our own standards are flexible, and over time they get more like the standards of our own culture to make it easier for us to feel good about ourselves. A much safer and sharper way to awaken conscience is by viewing ourselves in the light of absolute right and wrong. This is an important function of God's moral law. As Paul puts it in his letter to the church in Rome, 'through the law we become conscious of our sin' (Romans 3:20).

What Paul means is that our consciences become clearly aware of our sin through hearing God's law. An item of clothing may be dirty, but not look very dirty when it is in a pile of mixed coloured clothing. But place it against a bright white background and we see its dirt for what it is. God's law is the bright clean background which shows our dirt in all its ugliness.

God's method (if we may call it that) is, as one old writer put it, 'first, to wound by the Law, and then to heal by the Gospel'.[12] Real Christianity does not offer comfortable truths without first arousing and awakening the conscience to feel something of the terror of unresolved guilt in the presence of God.

Luther's contemporary and friend Philip Melanchthon asked Luther's advice about some people who said they had become real Christians. Philip was not sure whether they really had. Luther wrote to him that he should 'inquire whether they have experienced spiritual distress', by which he meant the terror of an awakened conscience. If not, if all their spiritual experiences were 'pleasant, quiet, devout', then Philip should suspect that they were not real Christians, even if, as Luther put it, 'they should say they were caught up to the third heaven'![13]

We must not become too rigid in insisting that real Christian experiences always come in a precise order. It is true that some people begin to get a flavour of what a wonderful thing it is to be a Christian even before they are very deeply convicted of their own sinfulness. Only later does it begin to dawn on them just how deeply they needed the Saviour they came to find and know. But unless at some stage there is at least a hint of terror in the presence of a holy God, a sense of real need for forgiveness, we have to ask whether their experience is real Christian experience at all.

One old statement of faith taught that when we think about the wonderful truth of being put right with God (justification by grace alone through faith alone), we must also think about what was called 'the conflict of a terrified conscience', since 'without that conflict it cannot be understood'.[14] Or, to put it another way, until I know what it is to be terrified by an awakened conscience, and to cry out to God for some way in which my conscience can be cleansed, I cannot really begin to understand the truth of being put right with God.

Faithful Christian ministry speaks to awaken consciences

The great task of awakening people's consciences is a mark of authentic Christian ministry. When pastors and ministers teach and preach without awakening the consciences of their hearers, there is something badly wrong. One fiery writer a century or so ago wrote that unless your pastor 'strikes terror and pain into your conscience' when he preaches, unless he 'makes you tremble . . . under the eye and hand of God, he is no true minister to you'.[15] He has a point. Unless Bible preaching and teaching brings conviction that I am a sinner in desperate need of forgiveness, it will feed my pride. But it is important that the preacher's conscience first be stirred and touched before he seeks to awaken his hearers: 'If the word do not dwell with power in us, it will not pass with power from us.'[16] In all this, however, we need to remember that ultimately, no matter how faithfully someone preaches, only the Spirit of God can touch a person's conscience.

J. I. Packer says that

> If our theology does not quicken the conscience and soften the heart, it actually hardens both; if it does not encourage

the commitment of faith, it reinforces the detachment of unbelief; if it fails to produce humility, it inevitably feeds pride.[17]

And the missionary David Brainerd wrote, 'I longed for the Spirit of preaching to descend and rest upon ministers, that they might address the consciences of men with closeness and power.'[18]

For the Reformers, 'conscience was the court in which God's justifying sentence was spoken'.[19] It is in my conscience, my awakened and terrified conscience, that I hear God's gracious word of justification in Christ. I do not just hear it outwardly and in theory; I hear it in my experience and self-awareness. This is an emphasis that is sadly lacking in some contemporary Christianity, and we need to recapture it.

Real Bible teaching does not make us think, 'What a clever teacher, how interesting to learn all that!' Instead it makes us say, 'Yes, I *know* it's true. I *know* I'm a sinner in need of God's grace; I *know* God is gracious. My conscience, my self-awareness in the presence of God, now tells me these things are true. I am humbled before God and cry for his mercy.' D. Martyn Lloyd-Jones, the great twentieth-century Welsh preacher, wrote that

> The real trouble with the unregenerate is that they do not know and understand the truth about sin. . . . The moment a man understands the true nature and character of sin he becomes troubled about his soul and seeks for a Saviour. It is the peculiar function of the law to bring such an understanding to a man's mind and conscience.[20]

Questions for personal study or discussion

1. How do you feel when someone points out something wrong you have done (as Sam did with his grandmother)? What choice do you face as to how to respond? What does 2 Corinthians 7:8–10 teach us about how God wants us to respond? What incentives does this passage give us, showing us the advantages of responding the way God wants?

2. Read the full story of David and Bathsheba in 2 Samuel 11 and 12. What do you think David was feeling in his conscience at each stage? Why do you think he finally came clean, confessed and cried to God for forgiveness? Why do you think David is convinced that the root problem is between him and God?

3. What do you think about yourself? Try to think of a specific example of a time when you have done or said something wrong. Where does God come into it? Is it really true that your wrongdoing is fundamentally a sign of something wrong between you and God?

4. How has this chapter challenged the idea that you and I are basically good people who mess up from time to time? Who do you want to blame for the bad things you sometimes do or say? Think about your own upbringing, family, schools and friends. Be honest! Who has treated you badly or contributed to your not being the person you would like to be?

5. Think about something wrong you have done. Think about the wrong deed itself. Then spend some time thinking about the roots and origins of that wrong thing. What led you to do it? What was going on inside you? Do some 'heart work', starting with the symptoms (bad behaviour) and tracing back to diagnosis (what is wrong with the heart). And then repent.

6. If you are a Christian, think about times when you have felt deeply convicted of your sin and have felt the pain of a troubled and awakened conscience. If you can never think of such a time, pray that God would graciously awaken your conscience and search your heart to show you more of his grace.

7. The awakened conscience is a work of the Spirit of God. Spend some time praying for your family and friends, that God will awaken their consciences to their need of a Saviour.

Notes

1. Charles Wesley, 'Lord God, who breathed your word of old' (quoted from *Praise*, Darlington: Praise Trust, 2000, hymn 555), verse 3.
2. The full story is in Nehemiah 8.
3. William Shakespeare, *Macbeth*, Act 5, Scene i.
4. Michael Wilcock, *The Message of the Psalms 1–72: Songs for the People of God*, Bible Speaks Today (IVP: 2001), p. 186.
5. James L. Mays, *Psalms,* Interpretation (Westminster John Knox Press, 1994).
6. *Richard III*, Act 5, Scene iv.
7. See appendix.

8. Alec Motyer, *Look to the Rock* (Leicester: IVP, 1996), p. 133.

9. Motyer, *Look to the Rock*, p. 127.

10. The great American theologian Jonathan Edwards argued that the source of human guilt was in our inclinations, not just in our acts: 'So Adam was guilty for his dominant inclination to commit the first sin as well as for the act itself' (quoted by George Marsden in his excellent biography *Jonathan Edwards*, Yale University Press, 2003, p. 454).

11. http://www.covenanteyes.com/.

12. Robert Bolton, quoted in Iain H. Murray, *The Old Evangelicalism* (Banner of Truth, 2005), p. 24.

13. *Luther's Works* (Fortress Press, 1963), vol. 48, p. 364.

14. From the Augsburg Confession of 1530.

15. Alexander Whyte, *Bunyan Characters, Third Series: The Holy War* (Oliphant, Anderson & Ferrier, 1902), p. 243.

16. John Owen, 'The True Nature of a Gospel Church', in *Works* (George Virtue, 1838), vol. XVI, p. 76.

17. J. I. Packer, *Among God's Giants: The Puritan Vision of the Christian Life* (Kingsway, 1991), p. 16.

18. Quoted in Murray, *Old Evangelicalism*, p. 30.

19. Packer, *Among God's Giants*, p. 141.

20. D. M. Lloyd-Jones, *Romans 7:1 – 8:4* (Banner of Truth, 1973), p. 114.

PART 3
THE CHOICE WE ALL FACE

6

THE HARDENED CONSCIENCE

Rob and his girlfriend Cassie were having a difficult time. Rob had said some negative things about Cassie in front of friends, implying that she was a bit thick. Cassie rang Rob the next morning and told him she felt hurt and didn't think his words were either kind or fair. Rob was really ticked off by this. He knew in his heart of hearts that she was right. But her phone call made him angry, miserable and bitter. He cut her off and stormed around his room in a fury.

WE'VE SEEN WHAT PAUL SAID to the church in Corinth (2 Corinthians 7:8–10) and considered the choice they had, the choice we all have, when faced with a guilty conscience. Paul's major emphasis was on the sorrow that leads to repentance and salvation. He thanked God that this was their response.

But he also speaks of what he calls 'worldly sorrow', and all he says about that is that it 'brings death'. This is the opposite in every way of the godly sorrow Paul describes. It hurts not for a little while, but forever. It does not lead to repentance. It is not the sorrow that God intends. It harms us. It leaves deep regrets. And it ends in death, both physical and spiritual.

We saw in chapter 4 that the experience of a guilty conscience is common to all of us. It always hurts and causes us pain, and we always want to alleviate that pain, to make it hurt less. If we will not go through the deeply painful process of having our consciences awakened so that we seek a Saviour, we have to find some other alternative.

This fact is so widely recognized that it has become the subject of jokes. The story is told of a man writing to the tax authorities,

> Dear Sir/Madam,
>
> I cheated the government in my last tax return, and have not been able to sleep at night since then because of my bad conscience. I enclose a check for $10,000. Yours, . . .
>
> P.S. If I still can't sleep, I will send some more.

Indeed, the *Oxford English Dictionary* lists the phrase 'Conscience money' as meaning 'Money sent to relieve the conscience, e.g. in payment of a tax previously evaded'.

We would love to be able to pacify our consciences without repenting. But we can't. Either we repent or we become hardened. Conscience warns us, and we must heed its warnings.

God's alarm

Ally had told a lie. Her dad asked her where she had been over the weekend. And she had not told the truth. Three days later as she walked to the bus, that lie came buzzing back into her head. She could hear herself saying it. Four days later as she tried to go to sleep, there was the lie again, bugging her like it would never leave her alone. She had to do something about it. But what?

Warnings are there to be heeded. I once lived next to neighbours who had a burglar alarm that kept going off while they were away. It used to make this ear-splitting noise that went on and on and on, even when – as was usually the case – it was a false alarm. On one occasion I got so fed up with it that I took my toolbox to the alarm box and disconnected its power supply. Not surprisingly, the alarm stopped. On that occasion, I had checked that no one had broken in to their apartment, so I hope my action was not irresponsible. But in general, ignoring alarms is a bad idea. It would be stupid, just because a smoke alarm sometimes goes off by mistake, to remove its batteries. Where I live in the centre of London, car alarms go off so often that most of us ignore them. And so they have become ineffective.

We've seen that conscience is God's alarm, alerting us to our wrongdoing and warning us that our wrongdoing will be punished if it is not forgiven. It is good that God has given us a conscience. Without it, other people could tell us about right and wrong but we would never know within ourselves that these things were true. Conscience is the point where the objective truths of right and wrong connect with the subjective realities of our experience, a God-given bridge between us and reality. The reality is that there is a living God who has given objective standards of right and wrong, and who will in the end punish all wrongdoing. Conscience persuades us within our hearts that this is true. It has been said that conscience 'is the only means we have within ourselves for seeing ourselves as God sees us'.[1]

And yet all too often we ignore the alarm. Not every quiet alarm is a safe alarm, and in the same way, not every quiet conscience is a good conscience. This chapter is intended to be a warning not to ignore God's warning. First we will look at five reasons why we may choose to go the way of worldly, rather than godly, sorrow. Then we'll consider eight ways in which we try to evade or soften the alarm call of conscience. As we do this, we will meet a number of the more notorious members of the Bible's 'Chamber of Horrors', people like the Pharaoh of the exodus, Herod Antipas, Pontius Pilate and Judas Iscariot. In each case we need to ask, 'How did they end up like that?' We shall see that a major reason why their lives ended in disaster was the rejection of conscience.

Five reasons why we reject conscience

1. The rejection of godly discipline when young

As Ben looked back over the last twenty years, he wondered how he had ended up like this, a heroin addict and now in prison for stealing. He remembered his mom (he had had no dad at home) punishing him for misbehaving when he was young, and then pleading with him not to start doing drugs. How he had resented her interfering with his life! And now it had come to this.

Proverbs 5 is an urgent appeal by a wise man to a young man not to go near a girl who is willing to sleep with him outside of marriage. Part of the warning reads like this:

At the end of your life you will groan,
    when your flesh and body are spent.
You will say, 'How I hated discipline!
    How my heart spurned correction!
I would not obey my teachers
    or turn my ear to my instructors.

And I was soon in serious trouble
   in the assembly of God's people.
(Proverbs 5:11–14)

Notice the words, 'How I hated discipline! How my heart spurned correction!' As we've seen, in the Old Testament the heart is very similar to the conscience. At the end of his sad life, this man will look back and say, 'In my heart I knew that the healthy discipline of my wise parents or teachers was right. But I rejected it. And that's why I have come to ruin.' Not all discipline is healthy; indeed, some parents and authorities abuse the young. But when parents and others seek to discipline us in line with right and wrong, they are God's representatives in our lives. And our consciences will bear witness within us that they are right. We must listen to this voice of conscience. If we do not, we will come ultimately to ruin.

2. *Being swept along by an ungodly culture*

Tyrel had been brought up to believe that sex was for marriage. His mom and dad really believed that. And so did he. Until he went to school and listened to the radio and read magazines and watched TV and went to movies. After which it was hard to believe it. You couldn't really believe it, he felt, without feeling stupid and out of touch. What a crazy, weird idea! And so he gave up believing it.

Writing to the Christians in Rome, Paul exposes the guilt of human beings by a careful and powerful argument (Romans 1:18–32). He says that we 'suppress the truth by . . . wickedness' (verse 18). That is to say, our wicked actions deaden our consciences so that the truth we know becomes a truth we suppress. We are guilty not because we do wrong, but because we *knowingly* do wrong. At the end of his argument he says, 'Although they know God's righteous decree that those who do such things deserve death' – that is to say, their consciences tell them that some things are wrong and deserve punishment, nevertheless – 'they not only continue to do these very things but also approve of those who practise them' (verse 32).

When a culture begins to affirm and approve wrong ways of behaving, the truth is suppressed and conscience distorted, so that we find ourselves doing wrong things without blushing. It is not difficult to see in recent Western cultural history that standards have changed. Just a few decades ago, when unmarried men and women began living together, there was usually some embarrassment, some expectation that people would think this was wrong. Now there is no embarrassment, and not even the expectation that normal people (that is, people who are normal according to our culture) will even bat an eyelid. The fact that 'everyone else does it', and that it is affirmed and approved in the media, makes it very easy to suppress the voice of conscience.

And yet it is very dangerous. The suppression of conscience has a narcotic effect upon morality. Our moral antennae go to sleep, and this can never be a stable state since we are always moving on to new (im)moralities. As Jeremiah said to a complacent people not long before disaster struck, 'Are they ashamed of their detestable conduct? No, they have no shame at all; they do not even know how to blush' (Jeremiah 6:15).

Parents are acutely aware of this as their children grow up. We begin with high ideals about the godly influences and environment within which we will nurture them. But before long, however hard we try, we find all sorts of other influences reaching them, and in what seems no time at all they are swimming in these wider cultural influences, which are immensely powerful. These influences soon drown out the voice of childhood conscience.

3. The fear of what will happen to me if I obey my conscience

> Simon was meeting his boss to discuss a discontented client. 'Why don't you just tell them . . . ?' – and then his boss suggested saying what was at best a half-truth, to pacify the client and make him think all was ok.
>
> Simon paused. He knew it would be wrong to say that to the client, because it was not true and was intended to pull the wool over the client's eyes. But appraisal time was coming up next month, and Simon really really wanted the promotion he had been waiting for. He knew that if he flatly contradicted his boss and refused to mislead the client, he would never get the promotion. That was how his company worked.

This third cause is closely related to the second but it is not identical. This is not just being swept along by a tide of perceived 'normality' (i.e. I would be abnormal, some kind of freak, if I tried to buck the trend). It is actually being afraid of what people will do to me if I follow what I know to be right.

'Fear of man will prove to be a snare', says the book of Proverbs (Proverbs 29:25) and it is so true. One of the most pathetic figures in the Old Testament is Zedekiah. Zedekiah was installed by the Babylonians as a puppet ruler in Jerusalem for the last decade of Judah's existence before the final destruction of the city and temple. During this period the prophet Jeremiah was courageously giving the people the bad but necessary news that they ought to surrender to the Babylonians. For bringing this unwelcome message, Jeremiah attracted some harsh opposition. In Jeremiah 38 we see what a weak man Zedekiah was. He alternately treated Jeremiah badly and tried half-heartedly to protect him. And yet – and here is the significant thing – when he really wanted to know what to do, he went and asked Jeremiah! So even while Jeremiah was his prisoner, Zedekiah summoned him and asked him what God had to say (Jeremiah

38:14). He knew Jeremiah was a true prophet; his conscience told him so. But when it came to the crunch, he was so frightened about what other people would do to him that he went against his conscience (Jeremiah 38:19). The fear of other people proved a snare to him, as it would later be to Herod (frightened of what his guests would think, Matthew 14:9) and to Pontius Pilate (afraid of the crowd, Matthew 27:24).

One of the most extraordinary things we learn from John's gospel is that many leading men in Judea actually knew that Jesus was the Messiah. So why didn't they say so publicly? John says,

> many even among the leaders believed in [Jesus]. But because of the Pharisees they would not openly acknowledge their faith for fear they would be put out of the synagogue; for they loved human praise more than praise from God (John 12:42–43).

Isn't that shocking? They knew – their consciences told them – that Jesus was the Messiah, but they never said so publicly because they were frightened! These leaders were actually slaves to their fear of people, and in particular the influential Pharisees (the religious 'storm troopers' of the day). Every time we fail to stand up for what we know to be right and true, because we are frightened of what other people will do to us, we harden our consciences and set ourselves on the path to the sin that leads to death.

4. The love of money

Megan had inherited a large sum of money from an aunt (at least it seemed a big amount to her, more than she had ever had before). The idea crossed her mind that she might give a proportion of it away. Ah, but on the other hand she could always trade in her one-year-old car for a smarter model. And book that luxury holiday. And build the conservatory. And if she was to do all those things then she couldn't really afford to give any of it away after all. She knew really it would be good to give a chunk away. But what about her and what she wanted in life . . . ?

Love of money is really love of myself. For love of money is really love of what money can buy, which is at root love of myself. Writing to Timothy, Paul puts 'lovers of themselves' next door to 'lovers of money' because the two are so intimately linked (2 Timothy 3:2). The wise man who wrote Ecclesiastes says, 'a bribe corrupts the heart' (Ecclesiastes 7:7). That is to say, it causes me to do something I know to be wrong in my heart, because of the benefit it brings to me (the bribe). It distorts my judgment, so that I do not do what is right. A cynic said, 'It is very hard to persuade a man of some truth when his salary depends on his not believing it.' I go against my conscience because of what I will get (or keep) in my bank account.

The most terrible example of this self-love leading to the unforgivable sin is Judas Iscariot, who betrayed Jesus. There is a revealing little cameo at the start of John 12. Mary, the sister of Lazarus, whom Jesus raised from the dead (John 11), loves Jesus with such gratitude that she pours over him a fabulously expensive jar of perfume. 'But one of his disciples, Judas Iscariot, who was later to betray him, objected, "Why wasn't this perfume sold and the money given to the poor? It was worth a year's wages."' And then John explains what really motivated Judas: 'He did not say this because he cared about the poor but because he was a thief; as keeper of the money bag, he used to help himself to what was put into it' (John 12:4–6).

Judas was the treasurer for the disciples. We do not know when he first helped himself, perhaps just to the odd coin from the common purse. No doubt his conscience prompted him, giving him a bad feeling before he did it and a bad feeling after he had done it. No doubt the second time was easier. Each time he ignored the voice of his conscience and stole some more it was as if he turned the volume control down, so that his conscience got quieter and quieter and caused him less and less pain. Until in the end he sold his Master for thirty pieces of silver. Love of money, which was love of self, led him to reject conscience, all the way to betraying Christ.

Love of money is not just a danger to rich irreligious people but a particular danger for disciples of Christ. Perhaps when Judas began as a disciple he was inspired by high ideals. But as time went on, the cost of discipleship (including the financial and material cost) was just too great. He looked at his relatives doing better for themselves and began to resent the sacrifices he had to make. Years later, when Paul writes to Timothy about the church in Ephesus, he has to warn him about religious people who have become 'people of corrupt mind, who have been robbed of the truth and who think that godliness' – that is, doing religious things, and especially church leadership – 'is a means to financial gain' (1 Timothy 6:5). This is why one of the qualifications of a church leader is not to be 'a lover of money' (1 Timothy 3:3). Every time our conscience prompts us towards generosity and away from selfishness and corruption, we must listen. Every time we reject these gracious promptings of God, we set ourselves on a very dangerous downhill path.

5. A gradual hardening of the heart

Jeff knew in his heart that Jesus was true and that he ought to throw in his lot with Jesus' disciples and become a real Christian. But it was so hard to do that at school because of the peer pressure. 'I know,' he thought, 'I'll become a Christian when I leave school. It'll be easier then.' But somehow it wasn't. And then at college, 'Maybe it'll be easier when I graduate. I'll do it then.' But somehow he didn't. Always he was going to do the right thing next week, or next month, or next year . . .

What the Bible calls 'hardness of heart' is the same as a persistent rejection of conscience: knowing in my heart that something is true, but deliberately not following that truth, at least not *now*. In some ways the most deceitful thing about hardness of heart is its gradual nature. It usually consists of a series of little rejections masquerading as postponements. And yet, as with all forms of addictive behaviour, each rejection makes it harder to turn back.

The classic biblical example of this is the Egyptian Pharaoh at the time of the exodus. More than a dozen times in Exodus 7 – 11 we read either that God hardened the heart of Pharaoh or that Pharaoh hardened his own heart. Both of these are true, and true at the same time. God is sovereign, and nothing happens in this world without his say so. So God hardened Pharaoh's heart. And yet at the same time Pharaoh hardened his own heart. God did not control him as we might control a radio-controlled toy, stopping Pharaoh acting as a responsible agent. If a radio-controlled car crashes into something and damages it, only one person is responsible: the person handling the radio transmitter. The car cannot be held responsible for what its controller has done. But with human beings it is very different. We make decisions and we are responsible for them. And yet – at a higher level – the decisions we make are the decisions that God has decided we will make.

God does not decide things 'on the same level' as we do; in that case, it would be an either-or: either God decides or we decide. No, he is God. And his decisions are at a higher level than ours. His decision-making does not evacuate our decision-making of moral responsibility. The fact was that the Pharaoh hardened his heart, making a succession of little day-by-day decisions not to listen to the voice of Moses when he was pleading with him to set the Hebrew people free.

No one decision seemed irrevocable. Each day he probably said to himself, 'No, not today. Today I will hold out against the God of Moses. But maybe tomorrow I will change my mind.' And yet, as he did that, day after day, plague after plague, warning after warning, one prodding of his conscience after another, his heart became set, so that the day never came when he would change his mind, and he had to experience the final judgment of the death of the firstborn. He would not judge himself, so he had to be judged. What began as an understandable and 'reasonable' reluctance to be bounced into a big political decision without sufficient supporting evidence became a settled disposition of the heart – set against the God of Moses.

This hardening also shows itself in a resistance to the voice of Bible teachers and preachers. At the time of the exile in Babylon, God said to his prophet Ezekiel, 'The people of Israel are not willing to listen to you because they are not willing to listen to me, for all the Israelites are hardened and obstinate' (Ezekiel 3:7). There was a rigid obstinacy that would not listen to God's voice through his spokesman. No doubt some of them rationalized it and said they just weren't willing to listen to Ezekiel, but the stark reality was that their hearts were hardened against God.

Looking back on the days before the exile, the prophet Zechariah said of the people of that day,

> they refused to pay attention: stubbornly they turned their backs and stopped up their ears. They made their hearts as hard as flint and would not listen to the law or to the words that the LORD Almighty had sent by his Spirit through the earlier prophets (Zechariah 7:11–12).

Of Zedekiah, the last king of Judah before the exile, we read that 'He became stiff-necked' – that is, he would not bow his neck in submission – 'and hardened his heart and would not turn to the LORD, the God of Israel' (2 Chronicles 36:13). And there are many other examples.

Pontius Pilate and his wife are a striking example of this hardening. Pilate knew very well that Jesus of Nazareth was an innocent man. Three times in John's gospel he says so: 'I find no basis for a charge against him' (18:38); after flogging him, 'Look,

I am bringing him out to you to let you know that I find no basis for a charge against him' (19:4); 'You take him and crucify him. As for me, I find no basis for a charge against him' (19:6). And as he sat on the judgment seat ready to condemn Jesus, his wife sent him a message saying, 'Don't have anything to do with that innocent man, for I have suffered a great deal today in a dream because of him' (Matthew 27:19). Her conscience gave her grief, because she knew that what her husband was about to do was wrong, and Pilate also knew it was wrong to crucify Jesus. And yet he went ahead and did it.

One way in which a hardening of heart shows itself is in not learning from our mistakes. God in his mercy gives us partial anticipations in this life of his final judgment at the end of time. His punishments and disciplines are intended to warn us so that we mend our ways. So in the time of the prophet Isaiah, God punished his people with a terrible war and invasion from the brutal Assyrians, and yet, 'they did not understand . . . they did not take it to heart' (Isaiah 42:25). To take it to heart means to listen to the voice of conscience, God's warning, the opposite of hardening my heart.

Sin is very powerful

So for these five reasons—the rejection of godly discipline, being swept along by our culture, fear of what others will do to us, the love of money and the temptation to a gradual hardening of heart—we may find ourselves going against what we know in our consciences to be right and true.

Sin in the heart is very powerful, and we must be realistic about it. The seventeenth-century poet George Herbert put it like this in his poem 'Sin':

> Lord, with what care hast thou begirt us round!
> Parents first season us: then schoolmasters
>   Deliver us to laws; they send us bound
> To rules of reason, holy messengers,

Pulpits and Sundays, sorrow dogging sin,
    Afflictions sorted, anguish of all sizes,
    Fine nets and stratagems to catch us in,
Bibles laid open, millions of surprises,
Blessings beforehand, ties of gratefulness,
    The sound of glory ringing in our ears;
    Without, our shame; within, our consciences;
Angels and grace, eternal hopes and fears.
    Yet all these fences and their whole array
    One cunning bosom-sin blows quite away.

How do some people make their conscience hurt less?

'It's all very well going on and on about my conscience,' said Clare, 'but the thing is that I really don't feel very strongly that these things are wrong. Maybe they used to feel wrong when I was a child. But they don't feel wrong now, or at least not *very* wrong. I think this whole conscience thing is overplayed, perhaps even made up by tiresome Christians who want me to feel bad about myself. But I don't, I really don't.'

Now we consider some common strategies for making our consciences hurt less when we resist them.

Strategy 1: Moral effort

Some people, troubled by a guilty conscience, respond by just trying harder to be good. In his book *Indwelling Sin*, John Owen speaks of people who are frightened by their guilty conscience into trying extra hard not to sin.

Being awed with a sense of the guilt of sin and the terror of the Lord, men begin to endeavor to abstain from sin, at least from such sins as they have been most terrified about.

This is a natural reaction. If my conscience rebukes me for some sin, then I must presumably try harder not to do it. And yet, as Owen points out,

> While they have this design in hand [i.e. while they are trying extra hard] the strength and power of sin begins to discover itself unto them. They begin to find that there is something in them that is not in their own power; for, notwithstanding their resolutions and purposes, they sin still . . .

In other words, they find that sin is stronger than they had first thought, much too strong to defeat by their own moral effort. In biblical terms, they discover in experience that they are under the power of sin.

And so, paradoxically, the renewed moral effort that was intended to make conscience hurt less, ends up with conscience hurting more, as the experience of repeated failure shows me as a moral failure. They are, as Owen puts it, 'ignorant of that only way whereby consciences burdened with the guilt of sin may be pacified – that is, by the blood of Christ'.[2]

Strategy 2: Escapism

Gareth is a very busy man. He struggles to juggle his relationships with his wife, his children, his elderly parents and his work colleagues. The only time he really feels happy is when he sinks himself into yet another soap opera or film, or plays endless games on his mobile phone. He enjoys these much more than the real world, which stresses him no end.

When Jonah ran away from what God wanted him to do, he boarded a ship and fell fast asleep. Even in the middle of a big storm, he slept soundly (Jonah 1:5). He managed to silence his conscience so well that he could escape into sleep.[3] That sleep is a picture of the escapism with which many in Western society run away from conscience.

This is an increasingly easy and popular option, and we can amuse ourselves to death.[4] Or we can spend our time in a virtual world, even a so-called 'Second Life', in which we create for ourselves a fictional and virtual identity. In this way we can pretend to be someone we are not and do our best to leave behind the person we are. Even social networking sites enable us to project ourselves as we would like to be seen, rather than necessarily as we are and as others see us.

Perhaps we never give ourselves time to sit back and reflect on our lives and behaviour. In this way I may hope to quiet my conscience when it nags me, sending it away as I might dismiss an annoying child, telling it to go away because I am busy.

Strategy 3: Blaming others

'It's all very well for you to point the finger,' said Dale to the minister. 'You had two parents together at home, a steady schooling and no money problems. I never knew who my dad was, my mom was an alcoholic, and I was out on the streets at fifteen. That's why I steal. So would you in my shoes.'

My family are great fans of the Calvin and Hobbes cartoons, which feature the boy Calvin and his pet tiger Hobbes. One of my favourites is a strip in which Calvin says, 'Nothing I do is my fault. My family is dysfunctional, and my parents won't empower me! Consequently I'm not self-actualized. My behavior is addictive functioning in a disease process of toxic co-dependency. I need holistic healing and wellness before I'll accept any responsibility for my actions.' At this point Hobbes says, 'One of us needs to stick his head in a bucket of ice water.' And Calvin signs off with the words, 'I love the culture of victimhood.'[5]

Conscience tells me it is my fault. But if I can persuade myself it is someone else's fault, then I can neatly shift the blame and get away from the voice of conscience. This is the great evasion of the so-called victim culture, where we are all victims and no one is responsible any more.

Strategy 4: Gradually desensitizing the conscience

Patrick and Jenny agree that Jenny will manage their family finances. When Patrick expresses surprise that they seem more hard up than he expected at the end of the month, Jenny lies. She does not tell him that she lost money through online gambling. The first time she lies, she feels very bad about it. But she soon gets used to covering up her growing gambling habit.

The first time Sean loses his temper and shouts at his son unnecessarily, he feels terrible pangs of conscience afterwards. He knows his shouting was because he is stressed, not because his son has been particularly bad. But gradually the shouting becomes a habit, and Sean doesn't feel bad about it any more.

Ignoring conscience gradually desensitizes this sensitive instrument. Paul writes about people 'whose consciences have been seared' or cauterized, just as human skin can be cauterized to make the nerve-endings cease to function (1 Timothy 4:2).[6]

A native American Indian in northwest Canada described his conscience like this: 'It is a little three-cornered thing inside of me. When I do wrong it turns round and hurts me very much. But if I keep on doing wrong, it will turn so much that the corners become worn off and it does not hurt any more.'[7]

There is a proverb about a woman who commits adultery, and then – in the vivid cartoon language of Proverbs – wipes her hands and licks her lips, like someone who has enjoyed a good meal, and says, 'I've done nothing wrong' (Proverbs 30:20). There would have been a time in the past when she would have blushed and felt guilty about her broken promises and deceit. But not now. The three-cornered thing has turned so much that now it doesn't hurt at all. Now she can be quite brazen about it. Her conscience has been desensitized.

John Flavel, in his marvellous book *Keeping the Heart*, quotes an older writer who describes the process like this:

> When a man accustomed to restraint, sins grievously, it seems insupportable to him, yea he seems to descend alive into hell. In process of time it seems not insupportable but heavy, and between insupportable and heavy there is no small descent. Next, such sinning becomes light, his conscience smites but faintly, and he regards not her rebukes. Then he is not only insensible to her rebukes, but that which was bitter and displeasing has become in some degree sweet and pleasant. Now it is made a custom, and not only pleases, but pleases habitually. At length custom becomes nature; he cannot be dissuaded from it, but defends and pleads for it.[8]

Paul uses the same idea of the conscience becoming desensitized in his letter to the church in Ephesus, when he writes, of people outside the people of God, that

> They are darkened in their understanding and separated from the life of God because of the ignorance that is in them due to the hardening of their hearts. Having lost all sensitivity, they have given themselves over to sensuality (Ephesians 4:18–19).

Repeated rejection of conscience (hardness of heart) leads to a loss of moral sensitivity, to a desensitized conscience.

Strategy 5: Rejection of the Bible

'You ought not to be resentful like that,' says Cara to her friend Debbie. 'The Bible says it's wrong.'

'Oh! The Bible!' scoffs Debbie. 'You don't still believe that, do you? Everyone knows that the Bible is just a mish-mash of religious inventions. Didn't you see that series on Bible archaeology which showed that a lot of it's fiction?'

Another way to quiet the voice of conscience is to take refuge with those voices that say that the Bible is a discredited or difficult book. We see a vivid metaphor for this rejection in a strange incident in the life of one of the kings of Judah shortly before the exile in Babylon.

The prophet Jeremiah has been preaching his heart out, warning the kings and people again and again and again that by their unfaithfulness to the living God they are placing themselves in terrible danger. This leads to him being placed under house arrest, so Jeremiah dictates his prophecies to Baruch, who goes into the temple and reads them out (Jeremiah 36). Some civil servants ask Baruch to read to them, and 'When they heard all these words, they looked at each other in fear' (verse 16). These words give them a guilty conscience and they are afraid of the judgment of God. But when they take the scroll to King Jehoiakim, he is not afraid at all. He is sitting by a winter fire. Every three or four columns of reading, the king cut them off and put them in the fire. By contrast with the others, he 'showed no fear' (verse 24). His conscience had become hardened. And very shortly afterwards, all the terrible things about which Jeremiah had warned happened just as he had said.

It is intellectually easy in our culture to mock the Bible's teaching about right and wrong. But it is also very dangerous. It is also intellectually easy – and lazy – to evade the Bible's challenge by saying it is a difficult book. But, as Mark Twain wittily commented, 'It is not the parts of the Bible I don't understand that worry me, but the parts that I do understand.'

Strategy 6: Self-righteousness

> 'The news is getting worse and worse,' moans Annabel to her friend Dave. 'Did you read about all that rioting and looting in London? How *could* people behave like that?' And, although Annabel didn't say the next bit, Dave knew what the implication was: 'Of course, *I* would never behave like that.'

If the first five strategies are common to everybody, the next three have a religious flavour. These are the strategies most likely to be found among those of us who go to church. We church-goers therefore need to pay extra attention to them.

The first is a complacent self-righteousness. We looked earlier at Paul's exposé of ungodly culture (Romans 1:18–32). By the end of the chapter we feel we want to join the chorus of disapproval of these terrible people, who not only do bad things but approve of those who do them, creating a culture in which these evils are regarded as normal. Very quickly we find ourselves with the Pharisee, thanking God that we are not as bad as those evil people out there in the big bad world (Luke 18:9–12).

This is why Paul goes straight on, at the start of Romans 2, from his exposé of the evil world outside to the evil world inside the church, the evil world of religiously respectable people who disapprove of evil while still doing evil themselves. His argument is devastating and cannot be evaded. On the one hand, we must disapprove of evil behaviour. If we do not disapprove, we line ourselves up with the people who not only do evil things but also approve of those who do them (Romans 1:32). And yet the moment we express our disapproval of those evil people, we make it clear that we know these evil behaviours deserve to be punished, and then when we ourselves do evil (as we all do) we are self-condemned. We have, as it were, signed our own spiritual death warrants by judging others.

Self-righteousness may make me feel better about my conscience because I can compare myself favourably with those I think are worse than me, but it cannot ultimately evade the judgment of God.

Strategy 7: Persuading myself that godliness is an external thing

> Archie went to see his local priest and asked how he could become a better person. The priest encouraged him to take Holy Communion two or three times a week, to get up early to say his prayers, to miss out on lunch from time to time (especially during Lent), and to put in place a number of very strict rules for governing his behaviour.
>
> Archie, who was very serious about becoming a better person, went away and did all the above. In fact each week he seemed to add another rule. He stopped going to films altogether. He decided it would be better to stay single and try never to think about sex. He always refused second helpings at meals. He got up early, first at 6 am, then at 5:30 am and then at 5 am. He bought a prayer book and went through it carefully morning and night.

Another way in which we harden our consciences is by fooling ourselves into thinking that holiness and godliness are external things. One way this shows itself is when religious people think that by denying themselves things they can become more godly. The technical word for this is 'asceticism'. This was what Archie was trying to achieve. The same kind of thing was evidently happening in Ephesus when Paul wrote his letters to Timothy. In 1 Timothy 4 he writes about people who were saying that we ought not to marry (presumably because if we deny ourselves sex, we will become better people), and we ought to abstain from certain foods (presumably because surely such food denial will make us better people).

We met these people earlier. Paul describes them as 'hypo-critical liars, whose consciences have been seared as with a hot iron' (1 Timothy 4:2). These people said that by denying things to ourselves we could become better people. But in their heart of hearts (their consciences), they knew that denying things to ourselves is not the same as self-denial, and that in our hearts there remain the same twisted mix of desires. Self-denial is denying myself to myself, a radical saying 'no' to all of my self-centredness. This is much deeper than a denial of some things to myself, which leaves me still at the centre of my little world.

We see something very similar in Paul's letter to the church in Colossae. He refers to people telling Christians 'Do not handle! Do not taste! Do not touch!' (Colossians 2:21–22). It doesn't much matter what exactly they were not to handle, taste or touch. The point was that they were being given rules, and it seems that the point of these rules was that they would suppos-edly make them better people. Paul says scathingly that 'Such regulations indeed have an appearance of wisdom, with their self-imposed worship, their false humility and their harsh treatment of the body, but they lack any value in restraining sensual indulgence' (Colossians 2:23). This externalizing of godliness is actually a peculiarly religious way of evading the demands of conscience.

Strategy 8: Repeatedly hearing the Word of God without repenting

Steve loves listening to sermons. He downloads them from all over the world onto his iPod. He listens to them while jogging. He listens to them in church. He blogs about his favourite preachers. He goes to conferences if big-name preachers are preaching. He laps it all up. He's a positive sermon gourmand. But those who know him well notice that nothing seems to change in his life or behaviour. His sharp tongue and bad temper continue as bad as ever.

Paul follows up his exposé of religious self-righteousness in Romans 2 by asking what has gone wrong. The people have been in church but have not repented. They have listened to the gospel of 'the riches of [God's] kindness, tolerance and patience' but have not grasped 'that God's kindness is intended to lead you to repentance'. They have stubborn and unrepentant hearts (Romans 2:4–5).

Every time we hear the law and the gospel of God, the voice of conscience says to us, 'you know these things are true; you know you are a sinner; you know God is gracious; you know you must repent of this sin today.' Every time we resist, we put ourselves on a path towards hardness of heart.

It is very dangerous to listen to the Word of God without repenting. It is a sobering thought that Herod Antipas was a great lover of forthright preaching, and there was no more forthright preacher of repentance in his day than John the Baptist. Herod loved to hear him preach: 'Herod feared John and protected him, knowing him to be a righteous and holy man. When Herod heard John, he was greatly puzzled; yet he liked to listen to him' (Mark 6:20).

Herod knew, because his conscience told him, that John was a godly man. He liked to listen to him. But when he listened to him, he did not and would not repent. He was in a relationship that John had told him was wrong. And in his heart of hearts he knew John was right. His conscience told him this. He knew he ought not to be married to his brother's divorced wife (Mark 6:17–18). But he refused to listen to the voice of his conscience. Every day he refused, he went further and further on a downward path. So much so that, some time after he had executed John the Baptist, when he met Jesus of Nazareth, Jesus refused to speak to him at all (Luke 23:9). He had so silenced the voice of his conscience that the Son of God was silent before him.

Danger alarm

Conscience is God's alarm in the human person. To ignore and reject conscience is therefore immensely serious, for it isolates us from a reality that will one day impinge on us, whether we like it or not. In the Corinth of New Testament times, the rich people in the church were behaving selfishly when they were with the poorer people (1 Corinthians 11:17–31). And they were being punished. We can't be absolutely sure how, but it seems that some physical sicknesses and even deaths were God's punishment. Paul says to them that 'if we were more discerning with regard to ourselves,' – that is, if we listened to our consciences, and responded to them with better behaviour – 'we would not come under such judgment' (verse 31). Either we judge ourselves now, listening to and heeding our consciences, or we will come under judgment later.

In his first letter, the apostle John says something immensely serious: 'There is a sin that leads to death' (1 John 5:16). There are sins that can be forgiven, but there is one sin that will lead inexorably all the way downhill to the grave and to hell. Jesus likewise taught that there is such a thing as the sin 'against the Holy Spirit' (Mark 3:28–29), a setting of the human heart and spirit so deeply against the loving movements of God the Holy Spirit that we will never be forgiven. This sin is the deliberate, conscious, persistent rejection of conscience. Conscience is what I know to be true. To reject what I know in my heart to be true is very, very dangerous. This was what Jesus' opponents were doing when he spoke of the sin or blasphemy against the Holy Spirit. They knew from Jesus' miracles that he was God's agent, and yet they

Conscience is what I know to be true. To reject what I know in my heart to be true is very, very dangerous.

deliberately said he was the devil's agent, rejecting their conscience.

Conscience, as we know, is a sensitive instrument. It can be desensitized so that it no longer functions as it ought, so we must listen to its voice before it is too late. Writing to Titus, who is leading the churches in Crete, Paul says of some people that 'both their minds and consciences are corrupted. They claim to know God, but by their actions they deny him. They are detestable, disobedient and unfit for doing anything good' (Titus 1:15–16).

There are few things worse than being a religious person whose conscience is corrupted, knowing the right thing to do but persistently failing to do it. Writing to Timothy in Ephesus, Paul tells of a terrible tragedy in which some people rejected faith and a good conscience 'and so have shipwrecked their faith' (1 Timothy 1:19). They looked like Christians, spoke like Christians, were perhaps even in leadership positions like Christians, but by rejecting conscience they rejected their faith and proved in the end not to be Christians at all.

The grace and patience of God

Gary came to see Richard, the leader of the Christian summer camp he had attended twenty years earlier. Richard remembered him – indeed, he had prayed for him from time to time over the past two decades – but he was surprised to see him again. 'I have come right back to faith in Christ,' said Gary. 'I heard the gospel at camp. I knew it was true. For twenty years I have gone against my conscience. But now I've come back to faith in Christ.'[9]

Before we move to our next chapter, I need to say a careful word about the grace of God. It would be easy to read these warnings and for any or all of us to deduce that there can be no hope for us. All of us will know of times when we have deliberately and knowingly gone against our conscience. Does this mean there is no hope for us?

Thank God, it doesn't. Simon Peter knew that Jesus was the Messiah when he denied him three times, but he was restored. Perhaps Nicodemus and Joseph of Arimathea were among the leaders of the Jews who knew Jesus was the Messiah but were too frightened to say so, and yet at Jesus' burial they wonderfully came out into the open as courageous disciples (John 19:38–42). Judas Iscariot was lost, but Simon Peter was saved. Caiaphas was lost, but Nicodemus was saved. None of us can say to another person that we know they have committed the sin that will lead inexorably to death and hell. None of us can say of ourselves that we have committed this sin. Indeed, the fact that we are anxious about it is a hopeful indicator that we have not. For those whose hearts are hardened are, by definition, those who do not care and are not anxious about these things. They are desensitized, calloused, cauterized.

An old writer helpfully distinguishes between a hardness of heart that a real Christian may have, and a finally hardened heart that leads a person to destruction. 'Total hardness feels nothing, but a Christian that has hardness of heart, feels that he has it.'[10]

If you are aware that there is a hardness in your heart against your conscience, and against the things of God, be encouraged. Your very awareness is a good sign. So this is not a chapter to lead anyone to despair, either about ourselves or about someone for whom we care and for whom we pray but who is not following Christ. It is not given to us to know who is a Simon Peter (backslidden, fallen, but to be restored) and who is a Judas Iscariot (on the road to ruin).

But we must balance this with treating conscience with the utmost respect and seriousness. Conscience is the bridge between the objective truths of God's law and judgment and our subjective knowledge of these things. To reject conscience is to threaten our spiritual lifeline—the way God, through his Holy Spirit, speaks to our hearts. It is like kicking the radio receiver because we do not like its message or disconnecting the fire alarm because we do not like its noise. A hardened conscience is a terrible thing. How much better to repent now, to pray for an awakened conscience and for grace to respond with repentance and faith in the blood of Christ, which alone can cleanse even the most evil conscience. There is no sin so bad that it will not be covered by the blood of Christ when we repent and believe.

Questions for personal study or discussion

1. Did you have good parents and healthy discipline when you were young? If you did, how did you respond?

2. Can you think of a time when you knew you were in the wrong, but just felt really cross and upset at being told?

3. What are the influences of culture (TV, radio, Internet, magazines, peer pressure, etc.) that make you feel that wrong things are 'normal'? Are there any particular issues in which culture cuts right across Bible truth today?

4. Can you think of a time when a love of money pushed you into doing something you knew to be wrong?

5. Are you postponing doing something you know to be right? It is not too late to change and do the right thing today.

6. Look over the suggested ways in which people try to make their consciences hurt less. Are any of them true for you? Have any of them been true for you? If so, ask God for his grace to enable you to turn around today and stop rejecting your conscience.

7. Pray for any friends or members of your family who are hardening their consciences at the moment. Pray that, like Simon Peter, they may wonderfully come to their senses and repent.

Notes

1. David Watson, *Know Yourself* (IVP, 1964), p. 13.
2. John Owen, *Indwelling Sin*, in Kelly M. Kapic and Justin Taylor (eds.), *Overcoming Sin and Temptation* (Crossway, 2006).
3. I am grateful to Maurice McCracken for this observation, in a sermon at Christ Church, Liverpool.
4. Neil Postman, *Amusing Ourselves to Death* (Methuen, 1985).
5. 21 Jan. 1993, Bill Watterson, published in *The Complete Calvin and Hobbes* (Andrews McMeel, 2005).
6. The word translated 'seared' may mean 'stamped with a brand mark that indicates Satan's ownership', just as a criminal or runaway slave would be branded with a hot iron. While this is possible, it is hard to see how a branding mark can have a worthwhile meaning when applied to something hidden like conscience. So on balance, it seems better to take the word in its other meaning of 'cauterize', i.e. make insensible to the distinction between right and wrong (the same sense as in Ephesians 4:18–19).

7. J. Oswald Sanders, *Problems of Christian Discipleship* (OMF International, 1958), p. 46.

8. John Flavel, *Keeping the Heart* (Christian Focus, 1999), p. 127.

9. This story is true, but the names have been changed.

10. Richard Sibbes, *The Tender Heart* (Banner of Truth, 2011), p. 41.

THE CLEANSED CONSCIENCE

This is the most important chapter in the book. Whatever you do, do not miss it!

Keith walks up as his two Christian friends Karen and Kate are chatting.

Kate: 'Karen, I can't understand why you are so joyful. I'm a Christian too, but I spend most of my life feeling terrible about myself. Being a Christian makes me serious about my failings and very miserable too. How come you're not miserable? Is it just that you don't take your failings seriously, or what?'

Karen: 'Oh, no! I know I'm a long way from being perfect. But it's so wonderful to know that I'm fully and freely forgiven. It makes me *feel* so good inside, so clean.'

Keith joins in: 'Frankly, I don't understand either of you. I certainly don't understand you, Karen. How can you take all your wrong stuff seriously and at the same time feel so happy inside yourself? It just doesn't make sense. And, to be honest, Kate, I can't see that being a Christian is doing you any good at all. It's just making you feel bad about yourself. I've got enough struggles in life without adding a religion that makes me feel bad about myself.'

Happy inside! A painful diagnosis for a wonderful cure

I was walking round an Ikea store looking for furniture for our daughter's bedroom, being assailed repeatedly by the exhortation to be 'Happy Inside!' The loudspeakers seemed to be telling me that Swedish flat-pack furniture could make me 'happy inside' – both inside my home and, presumably, inside myself. After reflecting, in my contra-suggestible way, that the idea was absurd, I thought, *the only thing that can really make me happy inside is a completely clean conscience.* That seems to be what Karen had. And it made her feel very good indeed.

When God gets to work waking up a man or woman's conscience, it is never his purpose to leave that person feeling miserable. An awakened conscience ought always to be on the pathway to a cleansed conscience.

So far this has been rather a depressing book. Although we started (in the introduction) by holding out the possibility of experiencing the joy of a clear conscience, most of our thoughts since then have pointed in the opposite direction. In chapter 4 we thought about what a guilty conscience feels like and how miserable it is. The guilty conscience keeps diaries, it makes us want to hide, it isolates us, it hurts us and makes us angry, resentful and restless, the very opposite of being happy inside.

And then things got even worse in chapter 5. There we learned that a guilty conscience is a symptom of a deadly disease. It shows we have a deep problem with God, not just with ourselves and other people. It is a problem that goes right back to when we were babies and reaches right down into our hearts.

This painful diagnosis is necessary if we are to put in place the treatment for a cure, just as it is essential for a life-threatening disease to be properly diagnosed if it is to be treated effectively. It is painful to hear the consultant telling us what is wrong, but it would be much worse not to know and not to be cured.

There are two parts to this chapter, an objective part and a subjective part. The objective part asks what Jesus actually did when he died on the cross. The subjective part asks how we may experience the benefit of what Jesus did. There is a bit of a paradox here, because in one sense conscience *is* a subjective thing (my consciousness of sin, etc.). And yet, as we shall see, our consciences bridge objective truth and subjective feeling of that truth, conscience being on the cusp between truth and feelings.

The objective truth: what did Jesus do on the cross?

We find crucial teaching about a conscience made clean in part of the letter to the Hebrews in the New Testament. This letter was written by an anonymous, and probably Jewish, writer to Jewish Christian readers (hence 'Hebrews'). One of the things the writer does a lot is tell his readers how much better Christianity is than Old Testament religion; in particular he shows them how real Christianity can make their consciences clean (Hebrews 9:1 – 10:22). He talks about this in four places:[1]

1. The Old Testament sacrifices 'were not able to *clear the conscience* of the worshipper' (Hebrews 9:9).
2. The death of Jesus 'will . . . *cleanse our consciences*' (Hebrews 9:14).
3. If the Old Testament sacrifices had actually made the worshippers perfect, then 'the worshippers would have been cleansed once for all, and would no longer have *felt guilty for* their sins' (literally, they 'would no longer have had *conscience* of their sin') (Hebrews 10:2).
4. Christians can draw near to God, 'having our hearts sprinkled *to cleanse us from a guilty conscience*' (Hebrews 10:22).

A guilty conscience is a symptom of being alienated from God

Max was talking about his crippling feelings of guilt arising from something he had done in the past.

'I know it was a very wrong thing to do and my conscience is always accusing me about it,' he sighed.

To which his friend replied, 'You know, I've been reading Freud. You need to learn that what you call your conscience is just a mismatch between your decisions in life and the values of your parents and others who influenced you in your childhood. It doesn't mean anything more than that. The best thing you can do is develop a confidence that your choices in life are valid for you, and break free from the shackles of your restrictive upbringing. Just because your parents would have thought what you did was wrong doesn't mean it was actually wrong for you.'[2]

The first question we need to answer is: 'Does a guilty conscience mean anything more than just a mismatch between parental expectations and our own choices in life, as Freud would have suggested?' Does conscience *objectively* indicate anything? It seems clear that the influences on us during childhood, especially from our parents, are enormously significant in shaping our sense of right and wrong; Freud was correct about that. But the key question is this: is our sense of right and wrong *simply* an internalization of the values of our parents and the culture in which we were nurtured? Or is there something more?

The writer of Hebrews answers this by talking about what seems to us some rather obscure stuff from the Old Testament. First, he reminds his readers how the Old Testament system of worship worked. They were Jewish Christians, so they were familiar with all this (Hebrews 9:1–10).

When we read through this passage it's easy to get distracted by the details (the lampstand, the table, the special bread, the golden altar of incense, etc.). But the key truth is actually very simple and vivid. When the people of Israel were travelling from Egypt to the Promised Land, they had to set up a big tent in the middle of their camp. This was called the tabernacle (which just means 'tent').[3] This tent had two rooms, rather like a big camping tent or a small marquee. And the critical thing to grasp is that you couldn't get into the second room except by going through the first. There was no back door to the second room; you had to walk through the first, and then through the curtain that separated the first from the second.

Now this two-room tent was a big visual aid in the middle of their camp so that they couldn't miss it. But what did it mean? The second room was called the Most Holy Place (in some translations, the Holy of Holies). It symbolized the place (the only place) where the living God was personally present on earth. Of course, they believed that God was everywhere, in one sense. He saw everything, knew everything and controlled everything. But if you wanted to know him, to be known by him personally, to be in covenant relationship with him (*covenant* was the technical term for this committed personal relationship), then you had to be in that second room. If you wanted to experience perfect beauty, completely untarnished, you had to get into that second room. If you wanted to know unfading love, unspoiled by unfaithfulness, you had to get into that second room. It was the only place on earth in which to find perfect peace, untroubled by cares, and perfect joy, unsullied by sourness or sadness, and lasting delight, unspoiled by fading and unshadowed by death. It was – in the vivid picture language of the Old Testament – a very wonderful place and the only place on earth ultimately worth being in, because it was the symbol of God's presence with his people.

So how did the visual aid work? Here, in the middle of their camp, was the presence of God himself. It sounds wonderful. But wait a minute. If you and I could have set up a webcam to watch the tent, what would we have seen? We would have seen lots of people going into the tent and coming out: the priests, the people paid and set apart to give us access into the presence of God. But if we had looked carefully, we would have noticed that, while they cheerfully went in and out of the first room, whenever it was their turn on the schedule, they never ever *ever* went into the second room. So that's really odd. They get close to the presence of God, but they never get into the presence of God!

When we ask the writer of the letter what all this means, he says, 'The Holy Spirit was showing by this that the way into the Most Holy Place had not yet been disclosed as long as the first tabernacle was still functioning' (Hebrews 9:8).

In other words, the whole point of the first room was to deny access to the second room! So long as the first room (the 'first tabernacle') was functioning, with its priests going in and out and offering sacrifices, it proved that the way into the second room had not yet been opened up (disclosed) and shown to the people. The first room shouted to every Israelite, 'You cannot go in there! You cannot go into the presence of God. Don't ever imagine that you can.' How often the priests must have looked longingly at that curtain that led into the second room. Wouldn't you have wanted to peep behind it? Just a peep. But they didn't dare.

And the reason why they didn't dare was that their consciences were still guilty. The writer goes on, 'This' – this whole system – 'is an illustration for the present time, indicating that the gifts and sacrifices being offered were not able to clear the conscience of the worshipper' (Hebrews 9:9).

Although the sacrifices could sometimes give a temporary and partial assurance of sins forgiven, there were always lurking doubts: what if I have sinned, perhaps in my thought-life, since offering the sacrifice? What if the sacrifice doesn't actually cover my particular sins? After all, when you study the book of Leviticus in detail, where most of the sacrifices are, you find that there were lots of things the sacrifices didn't really cover, such as 'intentional' sins. Always their consciences accused them and said, 'You cannot go in there; you are too dirty and guilty.'

And so the proper response to having that two-room tent in the middle of your camp was to realize that your guilty conscience did actually mean you couldn't enter the presence of God. It wasn't just a mismatch between what you did and what your parents thought was right; it really did indicate guilt and it actually prevented you from getting real access to God.

The writer comes back to this at the start of Hebrews 10, where the writer says that the Old Testament law (the whole system of the tabernacle, priests, sacrifices, etc.),

> can never, by the same sacrifices repeated endlessly year after year, make perfect [that is, make perfect in a completely clean conscience] those who draw near to worship. Otherwise, would they not have stopped being offered? For the worshippers would have been cleansed once for all, and would no longer have felt guilty for [have had conscience of] their sins. But those sacrifices are an annual reminder of sins (Hebrews 10:1–3).

Here's the logic: if the sacrifices had worked, then the worshipper would have felt completely clean inside. And then, of course, he wouldn't have come back to offer more sacrifices! What would be the point, when his conscience had been cleansed? But it wasn't. That was the point. In a way, the Old Testament sacrificial system was like dieting books and programs today: the only reason we keep buying them is that they don't work. If we found one that worked, we wouldn't keep coming back for more!

It must have been a sad job being an Old Testament priest. Perhaps they remembered the terrible story of Nadab and Abihu in Leviticus 10, who acted casually in the presence of God and paid for it with their lives. And so they had to be content with being so near, and yet so far, from the immediate presence of God. No matter how many good works you did, no matter how religious you were or how many sacrifices you offered, you could not go into that wonderful second room. That is what the whole system meant.

We too need to grasp that a guilty conscience is, objectively, a very serious thing. If I feel guilty, I dare not and will not enter the presence of God. For, if I have any sense, I will know that God is absolutely pure, and his burning purity will consume me. My guilty conscience warns me. It is necessary to grasp this objective truth before we can grasp and enjoy the wonder of a conscience made clean.

The death of Jesus removes the objective barrier between his people and God

George explained to me that he was conscious of a barrier between himself and God. He regularly attended Holy Communion and was a morally serious young man, but he knew that he did not really have access to God.

It would have been easy, and comfortable, for me to reassure him that he was imagining this and to say, 'What nonsense! God loves you. There is no barrier. You must be imagining it.' But it would not have been true. George was not (yet) a Christian. There was a real barrier.

Wonderfully, George listened as I explained the truth that on the cross Jesus Christ had paid the penalty for his sin and could therefore remove the barrier between him and God. He understood and accepted this truth, and the barrier was removed. From that day forward, George had access into the presence of God.[4]

You may have noticed that I left out something in my retelling of Hebrews 9:1–10. Something very important. I explained the general picture accurately, but with one omission. One man was allowed into the second room:

> But only the high priest entered the inner room, and that only
> once a year, and never without blood, which he offered for
> himself and for the sins the people had committed in ignorance
> (Hebrews 9:7).

Only the high priest. Only once a year, and never without blood. Any priest could go into the first room, whenever it was their turn on the list. They didn't need a sacrifice to go in. But the inner room was different. The whole business of the high priest going in on the Day of Atonement (Yom Kippur) is described in Leviticus 16. It was a tremendously elaborate business. And written all over the ritual was sin, sin, sin. It was 'an annual reminder of sins' (Hebrews 10:3).

And yet the fact that one man did have access was a sign of hope. It meant – and believing Jews grasped this – that one day there would be a high priest who would not only go in himself, but would open a way through the curtain for every believer to follow. Imagine a high priest starting to go through the curtain on the Day of Atonement, and looking around to gesture to everyone else to follow him in. He couldn't do that, and they knew it. It was more than his and their lives were worth. But one day a perfect high priest would do just that.

The writer tells us that when Jesus died on the cross, that is what happened. He explains it in terms of the Old Testament visual aid, like this:

> But when Christ came as high priest of the good things that are
> now already here, he went through the greater and more perfect
> tabernacle that is not made with human hands, that is to say, is not
> a part of this creation. He did not enter by means of the blood of
> goats and calves; but he entered the Most Holy Place once for all by
> his own blood, so obtaining eternal redemption (Hebrews 9:11–12).

The writer expands on this wonderful truth in the rest of Hebrews 9 and at the start of Hebrews 10.[5] Although the argument is complicated in places, it is a life-changing truth. But for the moment we will focus on the three key points the writer wants us to grasp and to which he keeps coming back.

A different barrier

First, the writer says that Jesus went through a different tent.[6] The Old Testament high priests went through the first room of a man-made tent into the second room. But that tent was only an illustration, 'only a copy' (Hebrews 9:24); the first room was not the actual barrier between people and God, but a visual aid to show us that a real barrier exists. This is why heaven (God's 'place', as it were) and earth (our 'place') are separated. Genesis 3:24 describes it in terms of God's garden with access guarded by angels with flaming swords. It is why men and women so often feel alienated from God. This was the barrier that George realized existed before he became a Christian. The 'greater and more perfect tabernacle' means the actual barrier between people

Jesus did in reality what the Old Testament high priests did by illustration.

and God (what the first room symbolized) and the actual presence of God (what the second room symbolized). Jesus removed that barrier: he did in reality what the Old Testament high priests did by illustration.

> For Christ did not enter a sanctuary made with human hands that was only a copy of the true one; he entered heaven itself, now to appear for us in God's presence (Hebrews 9:24).

A different sacrifice

Secondly, Jesus went into the actual presence of God not with the sacrifice of an animal, but 'by his own blood'.[7] In the Bible, 'blood' means life given up in violent death.[8] Jesus' 'blood' stands for his death on the cross, standing in as the substitute sacrifice for sinners, dying our death for us, paying the fair and right penalty for our sin. Jesus is God freely taking upon himself God's wrath. In an amazing sacrifice, Jesus *actually* takes away sin.

The writer comes back later and explains it in terms of Jesus' willing obedience to God (Hebrews 10:5–10). No Old Testament animal voluntarily offered itself for sacrifice; the very idea of a talking sheep or bull saying, 'Here I am; sacrifice me' is quite absurd. But Jesus said, 'Here I am . . . I have come to do your will, my God' (Hebrews 10:7, 9). The logic is this: God wants willing obedience from the heart. You and I have not obeyed and stand condemned. Jesus obeyed, and we are covered by his obedience. As Paul puts it, 'through the obedience of the one man the many will be made righteous' (Romans 5:19). The great hymn writer Isaac Watts captures this truth wonderfully:

> Not all the blood of beasts,
> On Jewish altars slain,
> Could give the guilty conscience peace
> Or wash away its stain.

> But Christ, the heavenly Lamb,
> Takes all our sins away;
> A sacrifice of nobler name,
> And richer blood than they.

A different result

Finally, the result of Jesus' death is very different from the Old Testament sacrifices. They had to be offered again and again, day after day, year after year. But because Christ's sacrifice was perfect, he entered 'once for all' and obtained for his people an 'eternal redemption' (Hebrews 9:12). The writer keeps coming back to this: Jesus Christ suffered once, and only once (Hebrews 9:12, 25, 26, 28; 10:12). In some ways it was an infinite suffering because of the perfection and deity of the one who suffered. And yet this infinity of suffering has been completed and never needs to be repeated. Christians remember it with thankfulness in the Lord's Supper or Holy Communion service, but it is never repeated.

And it achieves for his people an eternal, an everlasting, redemption. And this means a definitively cleansed conscience: 'How much more . . . will the blood of Christ . . . cleanse our consciences from acts that lead to death, so that we may serve the living God!' (Hebrews 9:14).

We need not, and cannot, add to what Jesus has done. We do not need, and are not able, to do anything more to have a cleansed conscience. Imagine going in to a famous art gallery with a child's paintbrush and paints in your coat pocket. You stand before some great work of art by Rubens or Michelangelo, quietly get out your paintbrush and – when the attendants are not watching – start adding your own touches of paint. When challenged, you say, 'Well, it's a lovely painting. But I thought it had a few bits missing. So I was touching it up. I hope that's OK.' No, it is not OK. You are ruining it! In the same way, I cannot add anything to Jesus' completed work of redemption on the cross without taking away from its value.

The objective conclusion

So there is the objective truth. When Jesus died on the cross, offering himself in perfect obedience to God, he did it in our place. He paid the penalty for the last sin of the worst sinner who will ever trust in him. He, the Son of God, took the righteous anger of God for the sins you have committed, the sins you are committing, and the sins you will commit, if you are a Christian. Every one. He has actually removed the barrier and brought you into the presence of God forever.

The subjective benefit: how can I feel that my conscience has been made clean?

Pat was singing away in church one Sunday morning, when he noticed a surprising word. They were singing an old Wesley hymn and came to this verse:

O for a heart to praise my God,
A heart from sin set free;
A heart that always feels thy blood
So freely shed for me.[9]

It was the word 'feels' that surprised him. What did it mean to 'feel' Jesus' blood shed for him? He had been taught to be suspicious of his feelings. But here was a great old Christian encouraging him to feel Jesus' blood.

In this second part of this chapter I want us to learn one main thing: We need to take the objective truth of what Jesus did for us on the cross and apply it to our subjective experience so that we believe it and begin to feel that it is true. This is the blessing of a cleansed conscience. Remember, conscience lies on the cusp between objective truth and subjective experience. So let's now look at how we can actually grasp, appropriate and feel the benefits of this rescue in life and experience.

Grasping the difference between the process of change in us and the perfection of what Jesus has done for us

Matt is talking to his youth leader at church.

'I am a Christian. I have turned from sin and trusted Christ. Really. And I think God is at work in me to change me. Often it feels like "two steps forward, one step back", or even "one step forward, two steps back". But, taking it all in all, other people whom I trust tell me that I am gradually changing for the better. And the more I change, the closer I feel to God.'

Most of us can identify with Matt's comments. So this is the problem: why am I expected to rejoice now about being close to God when the reality is that I ought to be struggling now to get closer to God (and maybe look forward to being very close to him in the future)?

Let's look at a verse from that section of Hebrews 9 and 10 that we focused on earlier in the chapter: 'For by one sacrifice he [Christ] has made perfect for ever those who are being made holy' (Hebrews 10:14).

Notice the surprise. Christ *has made perfect* people who are still *being made* holy. How can this be? Surely it would be more logical to say, 'Christ is gradually making perfect people who are gradually being made holy.' But he doesn't say that. The reality in your and my heart is that we are gradually – so, so gradually! – being made holy, godly and Christlike.[10] BUT – and this is the big thing to grasp – we who are gradually being changed have already been made perfect in the sight of God by the death of Jesus Christ. By his one sacrifice for us he has made us perfect, definitively cleansing our consciences so that we can follow our High Priest into the Most Holy Place, the presence of God the Father himself.

On the face of it, it would seem more humble to say what Matt says, that we are gradually getting closer to God. But it is actually very arrogant. It implies that we can get ourselves closer to God, and this makes what Jesus did for us on the cross pointless. It is like adding our pathetic touching-up paintwork to the masterpiece of Jesus' finished work on the cross.

The need to consciously reapply this truth to our consciences

Paul had been a Christian for some years now. He had been clearly taught the central truths of the Christian gospel. But somehow he never seemed to experience any great joy. It just felt like a formula he had learned. He knew in theory that he was forgiven, but he never really *felt* forgiven. He carried around with him a burden of feeling guilty about stuff from the past (and the present too), and he longed to be able to get rid of this burden.

In Hebrews 10:19–25 the writer takes all the doctrine he has taught from Hebrews 9:1 through Hebrews 10:18 and applies it to his hearers and to us. First (in verses 19–21), he sums up the objective truth. And then (in verses 22–25) he tells us what to do with this truth. All of this is important, but for now we are going to focus on the first application in verse 22. Since all these objective things are true, he says,

Let us draw near to God with a sincere heart and with the full assurance that faith brings, having our hearts sprinkled to cleanse us from a guilty conscience and having our bodies washed with pure water (Hebrews 10:22).

'Draw near', he says, and the tense means, 'draw near and then go on and on drawing near, again and again, day after day'. This is a paradox. After all, haven't we learned the objective truth that Jesus has brought us near once for all by his once for all death?[11] Yes, we have. What the writer means is that we should consciously enjoy and use the privilege that Jesus has won for us. He wants us, in our subjective experience, to enjoy the objective truth of access to God.

The reference to having bodies washed with water may be about Christian baptism, the outward sign of all that God does for someone when they become a Christian.[12] The 'sprinkling' is a reference to what Moses did with the blood of a sacrifice in Exodus 24:1–8. The blood had to be sprinkled as a way of saying that it was not enough for the sacrifice to be made; it had to be applied personally. This was the only time in the Old Testament when blood had to be sprinkled on people. Whereas their skin was sprinkled with the blood of an animal, our hearts need to be sprinkled with the blood of Jesus. The death of Jesus needs to be personally applied to our hearts and consciences.[13]

As we know, the blood of Christ makes us clean from all sin. And when by faith we believe this is true, our subjective conscious awareness of sin is transformed. Yes, we know that in our actions, our words and our thoughts we continue to be sinners. And yet, wonderfully, we are covered by the obedience of Jesus Christ, so that we can, with heads held high, walk behind him into the Most Holy Place with our consciences absolutely clear. When the Devil, who loves to accuse Christians,[14] points his finger at us and says, 'What, you? You can't walk in there', we can with absolute confidence and boldness say, 'Why not? I am justified. My conscience, which was so dirty, is absolutely cleansed by the blood of Christ.'

So never give up drawing near to God, says the writer. As he puts it earlier in his letter, 'Let us then approach the throne of grace with confidence, so that we may receive mercy and find grace to help us in our time of need' (Hebrews 4:16).

Making this truth our own by faith

It is an extraordinary and terrible thing that the exhortation to keep drawing near should even be necessary. I have been wondering why. Why do we, who have the right to enter heaven itself, need to be exhorted to do so?

I think the answer is that prayer is the expression of faith, yet by nature we, both today and in the first century, want prayer to be a matter of religious technique. If someone comes to me and offers me some spiritual technique to make me feel closer to God, and tells me this has revolutionized her prayer life, my ears prick up. Don't yours? I would love to feel closer to God. While working on this book I went through several weeks of struggling with a feeling of numbness in my relationship to God. I suspect this was partly exhaustion, partly stress, and partly just sin. But I would have loved to feel closer to God. In my heart I echoed the words of poor depressive William Cowper,

> Where is the blessedness I knew
> When first I saw the Lord?
> Where is the soul-refreshing view
> Of Jesus and his Word?[15]

If only someone could give me a technique, a spirituality of prayer to enable me to feel God's presence more!

And yet prayer is the outworking of faith. Draw near, says the writer, 'with a sincere heart and with the full assurance that *faith* brings', literally, 'with fullness of faith'. This means that we take God at his word. God says that the blood of Jesus makes us clean from all sin (1 John 1:7). Faith means believing that God means what he says. Drawing near to God is not a mystical experience, as if we would know we were near God when we felt we were near God. It is the expression of faith: I know I am near God because God says that when I draw near to him in prayer I enter the Most Holy Place by the blood of Jesus.

And as I take God at his word, then – one way or another – the feelings follow. Feelings of being close to God are wonderful things to have, and important too, but they result not from any religious technique, but rather from taking God at his word, which is faith.

It is important to be clear that this business of 'sprinkling' is not something we have to *do*. Just as the people in the Old Testament did not sprinkle themselves (Moses sprinkled them), so we do not sprinkle ourselves with the blood of Jesus, any more than a person baptizes himself with water. No, to exercise faith is to believe that God has already sprinkled my heart with the blood of Jesus. We believe and appropriate for our experience the objective truth of the sprinkling that God has already done for us.

So faith personally applies to our subjective experience the objective truth of a cleansed conscience. Wonderfully, I am simultaneously aware that I am a sinner and yet also I have been sprinkled clean and can go through the curtain into the presence of a holy God.

Reapplying the truth again and again and again

Now, as we know, this truth of a cleansed conscience isn't so simple in real life, is it? Someone has said that conscience is like a dog shut up in a cellar because of its barking, but always waiting to get back into the house to cause trouble.[16] The person who is not a Christian tries to hide it away in the cellar. For them, it is a good thing when they are 'dogged' by a bad conscience.

For the Christian it is different. When I sin, my conscience still works; indeed, if anything, it is more sensitive than it was before I believed. What I need to do is not hide it away in the cellar, but consciously remind myself of the blood of Christ sprinkled over me to cleanse my conscience.

I need to do that so that I will exercise my amazing right of entry to the Most Holy Place. So, says the writer, don't stop doing that. Don't stop believing in the blood of Jesus. And don't stop praying. Don't settle for a superficial imitation of Christianity, going through the motions. Don't stop actually genuinely entering into the Holy of Holies and drawing near in prayer on the basis of the priesthood of Jesus. That is an awesome privilege. Don't neglect it.

The fact that the cleansed conscience is appropriated (and reappropriated) by faith warns us against a morbidly introspective conscience that becomes 'so morbid as to refuse the forgiveness promised in the gospel'.[17] Such a refusal may look like a great humility, but it is not. Sometimes it is an arrogant determination to do for myself what is necessary for a clean conscience. Perhaps more often it expresses itself in a sense of despair, that I cannot manage to do for myself what is needed for a clean conscience. Surprisingly, both the despair and the pride have their roots in a reluctance to bow before the grace of God. Such morbid introspection needs rebuke, not affirmation.

In his first letter, John writes, 'This is how we know that we belong to the truth and how we set our hearts at rest in his presence.' He is writing about subjective assurance, setting our troubled and guilt-ridden hearts at rest in the presence of God. He goes on, 'if our hearts condemn us' – that is, by a guilty conscience – 'we know that God is greater than our hearts, and he knows everything.' So we trust that God knows our sinful hearts and means what he says, that the blood of Christ makes us clean. And as we trust that truth, our hearts find rest. And so he goes on, 'Dear friends, if our hearts do not condemn us, we have confidence before God' (1 John 3:19–21). So the process seems to be this: my (Christian) heart is condemned and troubled by a guilty conscience, I tell myself again the gospel truths of Christ's blood, and as I believe these truths afresh my heart finds rest, and then I experience again a fresh confidence before God. This is not a one-off process, but something that needs to happen again and again.

Learning to do this is important for Christian stability. If I am not sure about what Christ has done for me, I will always be dissatisfied with how I relate to God, dogged by uncertainty and insecurity. When someone (a peddler in the spirituality market-place) offers me a new technique that will cure my spiritual depression, I will be the first to sign up. If someone tells me about a church on the other side of the world where this cure is being experienced, I will save up and fly out there to get the cure, the 'new thing that God is doing', all because I will not believe what God says. Instead of wasting my money, I need to think about the new and living way Jesus has opened up for me into the immediate presence of God. When my heart is filled with the wonder of this truth, I will be oblivious to the attraction of second-rate substitutes.

So the death of Christ not only deals with the objective truth of our guilt before God, but also addresses our subjective awareness of that guilt. It changes not only the way we are before God, our actual status, but also our perception and our inward thoughts about ourselves. By faith we say to ourselves, 'God says I have been made perfect in and by the obedience of Jesus Christ. And I believe that what God says is true. I have been made perfect. I am cleansed at the deepest level of human personhood. Not only my actions and words, but my memories are cleansed too. So that when conscience drags up in my memory something of which I am ashamed, faith says to conscience that this thing, this sin, this impurity, this greed, this omission, this cowardice, whatever it may be, has been made clean by the blood of Christ. All of it.'

I take it that this is what John means in 1 John 1:9 when he says, 'If we confess our sins, he is faithful and just and will forgive us our sins and purify us from all unrighteousness.'

The Puritan William Fenner wrote about the blessing of a good conscience:

> We must use the assurance of faith in applying the blood of Christ. We must take trouble to purge and cleanse our consciences with it. If we find that we have sinned, we must run straightaway to the blood of Christ to wash away our sin. We must not let the wound fester, but get it healed immediately. As we sin daily, so he cleanses daily, and we must daily go to him for it. . . . Every day let us claim a daily pardon. Let us not go to sleep at night without claiming fresh pardon. Better sleep in a house full of adders and poisonous animals than sleep with one sin. Be sure with each day to clear the sins of the day. Then shall our consciences have true peace.[18]

This is what Wesley was talking about in the hymn earlier in the chapter. This is what it means to 'feel' the blood of Christ shed for us.

In his wonderful little book *Keeping the Heart*, the Puritan John Flavel has a section on how to keep our hearts at times when we are afraid, when, as he puts it, 'there are ominous signs in the heavens, or the distress of nations in perplexity, the sea and the waves roaring', when 'the hearts of men fail for fear', when we have 'fightings within, fears without'. In his typical Puritan way, he has fourteen answers for this! But listen to number 9:

> Get your conscience sprinkled with the blood of Christ from all guilt, and that will set your heart above all fear. It is guilt upon the conscience that softens and makes cowards of our spirits: 'the righteous are bold as a lion'. It was guilt in Cain's conscience that made him cry, 'Every one that findeth me will slay me.' A guilty conscience is more terrified by imagined fears, than a pure conscience is by real ones. A guilty sinner carries a witness against himself in his own bosom. It was guilty Herod cried out, 'John the Baptist is risen from the dead.' Such a conscience is the devil's anvil, on which he fabricates all those swords and spears with which the guilty sinner pierces himself. Guilt is to danger, what fire is to gunpowder: a man need not fear to walk among many barrels of powder, if he have no fire about him.[19]

It is a truly wonderful thing to know in experience the joy of a conscience cleansed daily by the blood of Christ.

Questions for personal study or discussion

1. Why do you think it has been important to spend so much time analysing our guilty consciences and what they mean?

2. Are you, or have you been, aware of a barrier between yourself and God?

3. In your own words, give a simple explanation of what Jesus did on the cross and why it matters.

4. If you are a Christian, why is it important to grasp that Jesus died once to pay the penalty for all your sins forever?

5. Do you ever struggle with knowing about forgiveness in theory but not really feeling that it is true in your experience? If so, how does the teaching of this chapter warn you what not to do about it and show you the right response?

6. How can we encourage one another to go on believing the gospel and feeling it to be true, so that we consciously draw near to God day by day?

Notes

1. These are four of the only five times in the whole letter where he speaks about conscience. The other is Hebrews 13:18. This concentration strongly suggests that a cleansed conscience is a major theme of this section.
2. This is essentially Freud's analysis. See appendix, snapshot 4.
3. Later this tent became a building, Solomon's temple, and (much later) the 'second temple' built after the exile in Babylon. But the architecture always had the same essential two-room structure at its heart.
4. This is a true story.
5. From Hebrews 9:11 to 10:18. See Peter T. O'Brien, *Hebrews* (Apollos,

2010) for a clear and scholarly recent treatment. For a fuller study of what the Bible teaches about the death of Jesus, see John Stott, *The Cross of Christ* (IVP, 1986) or Mark Meynell, *Cross-Examined* (IVP, 2005).

6. The writer comes back to this in Hebrews 9:23–24.

7. Hebrews 9:13–22 expands on this. Every verse mentions blood or death.

8. See Alan Stibbs, *His Blood Works: The Meaning of the Word 'Blood' in Scripture* (Christian Focus, 2011).

9. I have quoted from *Christian Hymns* (Evangelical Movement of Wales, 1977), hymn 690. It is interesting to note that *Praise* (Praise Trust, 2000), hymn 812 rewords the relevant line to read, 'a heart that's sprinkled with the blood'. Both are true, the objective sprinkling and the subjective feeling.

10. See Tim Chester, *You Can Change* (IVP, 2008).

11. See also Romans 5:1 and 1 Peter 3:16.

12. This is probably the meaning of 1 Peter 3:21, where Peter says baptism is 'not the removal of dirt from the body but the pledge of a clear conscience towards God'. This probably means that baptism is the outward sign of the cleansed conscience that God gives to every real Christian. Baptism does not guarantee this, but it does symbolize it.

13. Jesus alluded to this at the Last Supper. His words, 'This is my blood of the covenant', echo almost word for word the Greek translation of Exodus 24:8.

14. In Revelation 12:10 he is called the 'accuser' of Christians.

15. Hymn: 'O for a Closer Walk with God'.

16. Emil Brunner, *Man in Revolt* (Lutterworth Press, 1939), p. 202.

17. 'Conscience', in David J. Atkinson and David H. Field (eds.), *New Dictionary of Christian Ethics and Pastoral Theology* (IVP, 1995).

18. William Fenner, in J. I. Packer, *Among God's Giants: The Puritan Vision of the Christian Life* (Kingsway, 1991), p. 150. I have paraphrased some of the old-fashioned English.

19. John Flavel, *Keeping the Heart* (Christian Focus, 1999), p. 77.

PART 4
DEVELOPING A
CHRISTIAN CONSCIENCE

8

THE CALIBRATED
CONSCIENCE

WHAT DO YOU DO if you've been brought up to honour Sunday as a Christian sabbath, and you join a church where most people don't?

Or if you've been brought up to think that infant baptism is very important and you join a church where only adult believers are baptized? Or perhaps you are convinced that infant baptism is unbiblical and you find yourself in a Christian Union with Christians who firmly believe it is biblical?

Maybe you have been brought up in the Free Church of Scotland, where they used to think it wrong to sing anything other than psalms in Christian meetings and you move south of the border and join an evangelical church where they sing other songs and hymns?

Or what if you have been firmly taught that the King James Bible translation is the only reliable one in English, and you find yourself in a church using the New International or the English Standard Version?

Or if you have been brought up as a teetotaler and find yourself with Christians who enjoy a beer or a glass of wine with a meal?

How do you react if you have never been to an R-rated film, perhaps never even a PG-13, and you find yourself with Christians who see nothing wrong with watching one from time to time?

Or perhaps you have come to the conviction that it is wrong to shop at certain supermarkets because their policies seem unethical, and you find yourself with others who don't have that conviction?

We turn now to the question of what a truly Christian conscience looks like. I am not going to 'solve' the problems I've listed above, but we'll see some principles that will help us to grapple with them and others like them.

Let's go back to Corinth and Rome.[1] We'll focus on how our consciences relate to those of others, especially in a church, and also on how our consciences ought to relate to the Bible. So we will consider the social aspect of conscience (one another) and the religious aspect of conscience (God and his Word). There are five main things we can learn.

We influence one another more than we think

Jack has been brought up in a Christian home. He didn't used to swear, not because he himself was a Christian (he wasn't, or not yet), but because the air he breathed did not include swearing. But after a few years at school, swear words began to creep into his vocabulary and some of them slipped out at home by mistake. The air he breathed at school was full of swear words; they were as common as oxygen. He breathed them in, and now he began to breathe them out again.

The reason why Paul addresses the questions in Rome and Corinth is because they were dividing the church. We are not moral islands, making decisions all on our own, but are members of societies, communities, fellowships and social groupings. And our decisions are influenced, much more than we sometimes like to think, by the actions and words of others around us. This may be for good or ill.

Psalm 1 proclaims a blessing on 'The one who does not walk in step with the wicked or stand in the way that sinners take or sit in the company of mockers' (Psalm 1:1). The first chapter of Proverbs has a vivid example of being influenced for ill. 'My son, if sinful men entice you, do not give in to them. If they say, "Come along with us . . . "' (Proverbs 1:10–11).

We have already seen that fear of others, and being swept along by culture, are ways in which we are tempted to trample on our conscience and do what we know to be wrong.[2] We all know, most of us by painful experience, what it is to be carried along into doing something we knew to be wrong and later regretted.

Our influence on one another is clearly recognized in the phrase 'caused . . . to sin'. For example, several of the Old Testament kings are said to have 'caused Israel to sin' (e.g. 1 Kings 15:30). This makes sense only in the light of the influence that we can have on one another.

When Paul writes to Corinth, we might want to suggest to him, 'Why not just tell each of them to do what they think is right? After all, no one *has* to do what they think is wrong if they don't want to.' That is probably true. But Paul is much more realistic about the power of example. What happens when someone who is worried about meat sacrificed to idols 'sees you . . . eating in an idol's temple' (1 Corinthians 8:10)? In theory he says to himself, 'Well, he obviously thinks it's an OK thing to do. But I don't. And there's an end of it.' But it is much more likely that person will be 'emboldened to eat what is sacrificed to idols' even though he privately thinks it's wrong. Your example influences him, giving him a misplaced courage to go ahead and do something even though he reckons it's wrong.

In the same way, what happens when I and a 'weaker' brother or sister are having a meal at an unbeliever's house, and I am cheerfully tucking in to the meat that had been offered to an idol? When the weaker brother or sister points this out to me, he or she is watching with interest to see whether I will continue eating or not. If I happily keep eating, this influences them, making it harder for them to explain to our host that they do not think they ought to eat it. And so they probably join me in eating, despite a feeling of unease. My example has influenced them to do something they believe to be wrong (1 Corinthians 10:27–28).

In Rome, when the 'strong' go ahead and eat non-kosher food, they cause 'distress' to the 'weak' (Romans 14:15). It pains and upsets the 'weak' because they think it's wrong. In each of these situations, the behaviour of one Christian has an influence on other Christians. We must bear this in mind when thinking about conscience.

Love makes it easy for others to follow their conscience

The committee were discussing which movie they would watch at the next twenties' and thirties' group social evening. A well-known (and very well-reviewed) movie was suggested. The idea was greeted by a general murmur of approval.

But not from Hassan. He said, 'I think it's a great film. My wife and I saw it last week. But I wouldn't have wanted to watch it before I was married. It's not that it's pornographic; it doesn't actually portray anything explicitly wrong. But it would have been unhelpful for me and made it harder to keep pure in my thoughts and actions. I would have felt it was wrong. So, sorry to be a spoilsport, but I don't think we should view it at our group evening.'

The individualistic and selfish insistence that I will do everything I am free in Christ to do, whether it be eating idol food (in

Corinth) or eating bacon sandwiches (in Rome), is not motivated by love. If I love someone and I understand just how important it is for them to maintain their integrity by doing only what their conscience allows, then I will do all I can to make it easy for them to do that.

'Knowledge puffs up', makes me feel good about myself, 'while love builds up', that is, builds up the church (1 Corinthians 8:1). I will seek not my own good, but their good and their salvation (1 Corinthians 10:33). If I cause their conscience distress by my actions then I am not acting out of love (Romans 14:15). I will be keenly aware of the power and influence of my example, for good or ill, and will seek to use that example to make it easy for my fellow Christians to follow their consciences.

Our consciences need to be trained to submit to the Bible

Anita and Alberta were sisters brought up in a highly moral and principled family. When they left home they had pretty much the same standards in life. But Anita never settled in a Bible-teaching church. After a while she gave up going to church altogether. Alberta, however, settled in a church where the Bible was opened and taught week by week.

Before long, their views of right and wrong began to diverge. Anita thought of her conscience as a kind of personal monitor to keep an eye on her behaviour; she never wanted to do what she felt to be wrong. Alberta, on the other hand, found that week by week her ideas of right and wrong were being changed by the Bible. Anita's ideas drifted, and her conscience drifted with her. Alberta's were more like a boat attached to an anchor; when the boat drifted, it kept being pulled back to the anchor.

We saw in chapter 2 that both in Rome and in Corinth the Bible gives clear teaching. In Rome it is that all foods are now 'clean' and so it is all right for Christians to eat non-kosher food. In Corinth the issue is that idols do not really exist, and so it is not wrong for Christians to eat food that has been offered to these non-existent beings. Presumably Paul hopes that in both churches this teaching will gradually take root.

Our unreliable consciences ought to be deliberately and consciously subject to the reliable Word of God. There is such a thing as the tyranny of the weak conscience in a church. This is where people who are actually wrong cling so tenaciously to the preciousness of their (misguided) conscience that they will never learn anything else. 'Oh,' they say in a prissy voice, 'you mustn't trouble my conscience! I am very protective of my precious conscience!' And so they end up making an idol out of their conscience.

Paul says, 'Each of them should be fully convinced in their own mind' (Romans 14:5). He does not want anyone to do something while convinced in their own mind that it is wrong. That would be sinful. But it is also sinful if I treat the conviction of my own mind as my ultimate authority. As well as telling those who have understood the Bible not to strong-arm the others into doing something they think is wrong, in both Rome and Corinth he spells out very clearly what the Bible actually teaches.

Now presumably, when the apostle writes these things, he hopes those with weak consciences will be listening! He hopes that what he says will, gradually but surely, change the conviction of their minds, so that the time comes when they happily eat non-kosher food in Rome and meat sacrificed to idols in Corinth. He is not envisaging a stalemate, a tyranny of the weak consciences, so that hundreds of years later Christians are still eating only kosher food. No, he wants our consciences to be in a constant process of recalibration, so that they get more and more closely aligned with the Word of God.

He says to the 'strong', don't strong-arm people, but change them by patient teaching and prayer. And he says to the weak, listen to the Bible, listen to the teaching of the apostles, and let your conscience be brought more and more into line with truth.

That's why Luther stood his ground so courageously at the Diet of Worms when he asserted, 'To go against conscience is neither right nor safe'. He based his argument firmly on Scripture and said, 'My conscience is captive to the word of God.'[3]

This recalibration takes time to get deep inside us

We need to so soak our minds and hearts in Scripture that our consciences are progressively calibrated according to God's Word and our convictions are deeply internalized. Richard Baxter wrote,

> There is a dangerous error grown too common in the world that a man is bound to do every thing which his conscience telleth him is the will of God; and that every man must obey his conscience, as if it were the lawgiver of the world; whereas, indeed, it is not ourselves, but God, that is our lawgiver. And conscience is . . . appointed . . . only to discern the law of God, and call upon us to observe it; and an erring conscience is not to be obeyed, but to be better informed.[4]

The story is told of a well-known painter who used to keep a number of highly coloured stones on a shelf in his studio—an emerald, a ruby, and so on. When asked why, he said, 'All day long I am working at my canvas with mixed, impure colours, and my eye is apt to lose its keenness. So every now and then I stop working and feast my eyes upon these stones. And my sense of colour is restored.'

We are a little like that painter: when we feast our spiritual eyes on Scripture our moral vision is sharpened and restored.

We live in a morally muddy world and there are many influences on us that will give us morally muddied vision. Only the Word of God can recalibrate our consciences.

This is much more than just finding 'Bible answers' to guidance or decision-making questions. There is a place for that, but it can be a superficial exercise. Soaking ourselves in Scripture, feasting our eyes on it and meditating day and night on it, will give us much more than answers to questions; it will gradually shape our character according to the virtues of Scripture, so that we become the kind of people who will make godly decisions because our consciences are being lined up with the will and desires of God.

The calibration of the conscience is a ministry of the Holy Spirit. Just as the Holy Spirit first awakens the conscience, so he progressively calibrates it as he shines his light on the pages of Scripture and into our darkened hearts. Paul ties together the witness of his conscience and the work of the Holy Spirit in his heart when he says, 'my conscience confirms [what he has just said] through the Holy Spirit' (Romans 9:1). This is not just conscience as a private monitor, but a conscience being shaped and sharpened by the Holy Spirit.

The Holy Spirit works in us so that we actively learn and calibrate our consciences. As the writer to the Hebrews puts it, it is a mark of mature and growing Christians that 'by constant use' they 'have trained themselves to distinguish good from evil' (Hebrews 5:14).

We need to train ourselves, both by this soaking ourselves in Scripture and by constant practice in godly decision-making, so that our consciences are recalibrated to distinguish good from evil. This is a transformation in which we conform less and less to the moral muddiness of this world and experience the renewing of our minds (Romans 12:2). As a result we will learn to 'discern what is best' (Philippians 1:10).

The Holy Spirit does this work in two ways. Sometimes the Word of God will enable us happily to enjoy freedom in Christ in ways in which we thought we were not allowed. At other times that same Word will show us that behaviours or attitudes we thought were fine really are not fine at all. We will look at these two processes next.

Bringing the over-sensitive conscience into freedom in Christ

Kate had the kind of personality that loved detail and really wanted to get everything right. She loved it when things were in their place and when stuff happened as it was supposed to. She brought this personality into her Christian life. She really wanted to get it all right, exactly right.

The trouble was that, again and again, she worried about all sorts of little decisions – which route to walk to work, which order to do the jobs on her list, what exactly to say to her boss, how to put things right with her dad – so much that she was always worrying that she was doing something wrong. And of course when it came to the bigger decisions – like what to say when Ben asked her to marry him – she was in a terrible state. Her conscience was like a compass gone manic in a magnet factory. All she knew was that she would end up worrying, whatever she decided.

For some of us, especially those brought up in churches dominated by a repressive legalism, there is a need to be brought into liberty in Christ. In some ways, a legalistic church breeds Christians who are living with at least one foot in the old covenant world of Judaism; they are governed by rules that go well beyond the moral judgments of Scripture.

In this category too will fall some who by temperament lie towards the obsessive-compulsive end of the spectrum. These people like to have all the loose ends tied up, the 'i's dotted and the 't's crossed. We (and I write as one such) are always going to be liable to want to do what the Pharisees did with the law of

Moses: put a fence around it and, if in any doubt about what it meant, hedge it about with some extra regulations. We feel a lot safer that way.

If that is you, then make it your aim to submit your conscience to Scripture, and so to understand your freedom in Christ that you can joyfully and with conviction enter into that freedom. You will do well to ask the advice of two or three older Christians. They may well be able to give you a more balanced perspective and perhaps help you see that your misgivings are the result of an over-sensitive conscience. As in every other area of the Christian life, we are not asked to live solo; we need one another to help us see things straight.

There is a big difference between trampling on your conscience (doing something you really believe to be wrong), and educating your conscience. You may well need to do something that still makes you *feel* uneasy; it would be surprising if that were not the case, given perhaps a long history of avoiding it. But if you are now convinced from Scripture, with the help of wise friends, that it is allowed to you in Christ, and your conscience has been educated in that way, then you can do it without any danger to your spiritual walk and discipleship.

Sharpening up the under-sensitive conscience into godliness

Andrew used to think that tearing others down, and a bit of grumbling about them, was just normal and OK. Everybody did it. It was after all the staple diet of office chat. But after he became a Christian he began to realize that, although it might be normal, it was not OK. Gradually his conscience moved so that it set alarm bells ringing when he joined in that sort of chatter.

Colette had got into the habit of checking her email and surfing the net while talking to people on the phone. In fact she had become quite adept at making sure they didn't notice (turning the sound off on her laptop, and so on). But yesterday a friend was pouring out her heart on the phone about a very distressing relational issue. As Colette tried to (half) listen while reading her email, her conscience began to prick her. It wasn't that she had found a verse in the Bible that told her not to do it (there isn't one!); it was just that she had been soaked in stuff about really loving other people and she realized that not giving her friend her full attention was not loving her.

Paul and Debbie had been married for twenty years. While out for meals with friends, Paul had got into the habit of teasing Debbie and having fun at her expense, sometimes being very critical of her. They had got used to it as a way of relating, and Debbie kept her hurt feelings to herself. But after Paul came to faith in Christ, his conscience began to show him that this was unkind. Yes, he still slipped into the old ways from time to time, but now he felt bad about it and apologized to her. Gradually he did it less and less.

James used to stop off at the pub for a drink or two to unwind after work before getting home to help Susanne with the children's bedtime. Before he had become a Christian, the 'drink or two' had grown to an hour or more. By the time he got home, bedtime was over and he wasn't much use. But now he realized he was being selfish, and his conscience pricked him to get home sooner and help out.

Today I think that more of us suffer from an under-sensitive conscience than an over-sensitive one. We need to have our under-sensitive consciences sharpened up by the Holy Spirit. The corrosive influence of our culture, and one or two generations of Christian culture reacting against old legalisms, have made us lackadaisical about following our consciences. (I will say more about this in the final chapter, but a regular dose of careful self-examination under Scripture never comes amiss.)

Rather than assuming that all the behaviours of our Christian sub-culture are really godly, we ought to test them routinely against our daily Bible reading, our Bible studies and the preaching we hear in church. If we find they are not as godly as we thought, we need the courage both to change our own behaviour and to use the power of our example to help others to change.

Some of us may find ourselves oscillating between an over-sensitive and an under-sensitive conscience. We must all make it our aim to be realistic about the provisional and unreliable nature of our consciences and the ongoing need for them to be calibrated by the Word of God. The critical point that Paul makes is that our outward actions ought to spring from inward convictions. There ought to be no superficiality about us, no disjunction between what we believe and how we behave, no action that contradicts our conscience. Truth needs to be deeply internalized and then consistently lived.

Truth needs to be deeply internalized and then consistently lived.

Church leaders must be realistic about how long recalibration takes

> Terry had become senior minister of a well-known and long-established Bible-teaching church. He was looking forward to leading such a mature church, whose members would by now be so clear about Christian truth – or so he thought.

In his second week, there was some controversy when a national church leader publicly said that it was fine for couples to live together without being married. Terry was discussing this with his church council and was alarmed and surprised when one man, who had been in the church for fifteen years, said that he rather agreed with the national leader.

Paul commends church leaders whose work is preaching and teaching (1 Timothy 5:17). He himself toiled strenuously at this work (Colossians 1:28–29). It is only by preaching and teaching, in the context of fervent and faithful prayer, that godly convictions are formed and godly behaviour deeply developed. It is very easy to mistake a superficial conformity to Christian sub-culture for the deep convictions that come from a taught conscience over many years.

Paul does not want the churches in Corinth or Rome to change their behaviour as a result of peer pressure. This can happen all too easily. Every church has a culture, and when we join one we naturally fit into the culture, moral chameleons that we are. We look at the generally good behaviour we see and naively assume this behaviour springs from deep convictions, that each is doing only what he or she is fully convinced about in his or her own mind. How wrong we can be!

Paul longs for his churches to be shaped into the image of Christ, not by peer pressure but by patient teaching and prayer. I think this is why he specifies that deacons 'must keep hold of the deep truths of the faith with a clear conscience' (1 Timothy 3:9). They must be marked by integrity, holding deep truths with a life that is deeply consistent, with beliefs and behaviour arising out of deep conviction.

At the start of his first letter to Timothy, Paul reminds him that the charge to the pastor (the pastoral charge, the goal to which the pastor strives) is 'love, which comes from a pure heart and a good conscience and a sincere faith' (1 Timothy 1:5).

Sincerity is the theme of these three overlapping characteristics: a pure (or genuine) heart, a good (or clear) conscience and a sincere faith.[5]

Deep genuineness and authenticity come from a heart that is single and pure, not divided and mixed; from a conscience that is good, cleansed and clean rather than guilty; and from a faith that is real. This is the root and origin of all true love towards God and people. A good conscience is possible only where there is genuine faith, for it is only the blood of Christ that can cleanse the conscience. This is why Paul sets a good conscience alongside genuine faith here, and also later in the chapter, with the words 'holding on to faith and a good conscience' (1 Timothy 1:19).

Questions for personal study or discussion

1. Can you think of any times in your life when you have thought something to be wrong but others (perhaps Christians) have considered it OK? Or the other way around?

2. Have you ever felt pressured to do something you thought to be wrong? Can you think of ways in which you might have pressured others?

3. How have your views of right and wrong changed under the influence of other people around you? Are you aware of ways in which your own behaviour has influenced other people?

4. Have your convictions about right and wrong been changed by the Bible? Which convictions? Anything you thought was wrong that you now understand to be allowable? Or something you felt was OK but you now see is not?

Notes

1. See chapter 2.
2. See chapter 6.
3. Quoted in J. I. Packer, *Among God's Giants: The Puritan Vision of the Christian Life* (Kingsway, 1991), p. 140.
4. Richard Baxter, *Works* (George Virtue, 1838), vol. I, p. 115.
5. William D. Mounce, *Pastoral Epistles*, Word Biblical Commentary (Nelson, 2000), on 1 Timothy 1:5.

9

THE CLEAR CONSCIENCE

Adam, Annie and Archie were enjoying a coffee together and – for some reason – were discussing some rather deep issues.

Adam: 'I keep a personal diary. It's not just about the things I've done, the stuff you might put on a blog or Facebook, with photos and stuff. It's about the state of my heart. I try to think each day about what's been going on in my heart. I look into my heart and soul a bit and say sorry to God about this and that, and resolve to be different in future – that kind of stuff.'

Annie: 'Wow! That's a revelation to us, Adam. We do love you, but what an *odd* sort of thing to do. You don't strike me as a morbid introvert, but all this looking into your heart stuff . . . well, it just feels a bit weird to me. You don't mind my saying that, I hope. I know you're a Christian and all that, but why bother? I bumble along happily enough in my life without worrying too much what's going on inside me.'

Archie: 'Hmm. I can't make heads or tails of you either, Adam, but for a different reason. Annie, I would hate you to think that if you become a Christian you would have to become like Adam. I'm a Christian. But I don't bother about all that inward-looking stuff at all. I just think it's fantastic to be forgiven for everything anyway, without having to worry about all this self-examination stuff.'

Do you know the joy of a clear conscience? That was the question with which we started this book. Could you end each day with the words, 'I have a clear conscience'? In this final chapter I want to pull all the threads together and end by seeing how it is possible for us to live each day with a clear conscience. It will take effort, but it is well worth the trouble.

It was a clear conscience that enabled Job to persevere patiently through his troubles, and a clear conscience that emboldened Stephen to face martyrdom with courage.

Listen to a very striking statement that the apostle Paul made: 'So I strive always to keep my conscience clear before God and man' (Acts 24:16).[1]

Keeping a clear conscience is very similar to guarding the heart, as in the Proverb that says, 'Above all else, guard your heart, for everything you do flows from it' (Proverbs 4:23).

A guarded heart and a clear conscience are wonderful things. It was a clear conscience that enabled Job to persevere patiently through his troubles, and a clear conscience that emboldened Stephen to face martyrdom with courage.

The word 'strive' means something like 'take pains' (ESV). It conveys an almost troublesome attentiveness, a need for regular examination of life, the sort of thing that Adam did. It indicates that keeping a clear conscience is 'a definite task which fully occupies him from morning to night in all the situations in which he has dealings with God and man'.[2]

And the obvious question to ask first is: 'Why bother? If it takes pain and striving, why bother with it?' There are at least two quarters from which this objection could come, as we have seen from Annie and Archie.

First, a non-Christian (Annie) could say, 'Sure, a clear conscience might be a nice thing to have, but it is a bother. And I find it is not too difficult to suppress my conscience, in a sense to turn the volume down so that it doesn't trouble me very much. That's not all that hard and involves very little pain or striving. So I think I'll do that, if you don't mind.'

Second, there is a specifically Christian objection (Archie), which runs like this: 'I thought the wonderful thing about being a Christian was that I am fully forgiven anyway, so what's all this about the daily bother of keeping my conscience clear? Besides, I'm not very good at keeping it clear. So I think I'm not really going to bother with this and I will just trust in Christ to save me anyway.'

In this chapter we will see why we ought to bother and what taking pains to keep a clear conscience means and does not mean. Then we will tease out more fully what it means in practice by looking at the two ingredients to keeping a clear conscience.

Why bother with a clear conscience?

A clear conscience is the only safe way to face life after death

Clive was dying. He knew he was dying. As he lay in his hospital bed, his old friend and pastor Hugh was talking with him. Both of them knew it would probably be their final talk on earth. They chatted about their families. They shared some memories.

And then Hugh asked, 'Clive, is there anything you need to confess to God before you die? Would it help you to confess it now along with me as we pray together?'

Clive thought for a moment, smiled contentedly and said, 'No, there is nothing. I have done many, many wrong things. I have said all sorts of bad things. I have thought even more evil things. But you know, I have nothing whatever to confess. I have confessed to other people wherever I could the things I have done against them; I have done my best to put them right when it was within my power. I have confessed to God daily for years now and repented of every known sin. And I have made a habit of trusting anew each evening in the blood of Christ shed for all my sin. So thanks for asking but no, there's nothing. Isn't that wonderful? I feel ready to die. Actually, you know, I have been ready to die every night for many years now, thank God.'

As Hugh left the hospital, he did so with a smile on his face, deeply sad because he would miss Clive, but even more deeply happy for Clive. And he resolved that he too would be able to say the same thing when the time came for him to die.

Could you and I die like that? Today, tonight? In spite of knowing and honestly admitting all our daily failures? Would Good-Conscience meet us, as he met Mr. Honest in *The Pilgrim's Progress*, on the edge of the River Jordan, and help us over to the other side?[3]

Paul makes a remarkable statement near the end of the book of the Acts of the Apostles, which tells the story of the very early days of the Christian church. He is accused by some of his fellow Jews of breaking the Jewish law in the Jerusalem temple. At this point in the story his case is going to be heard by Felix, a Roman governor. Some Jewish leaders bring 'their charges against Paul before the governor' (Acts 24:1). They make the accusation: 'We have found this man to be a troublemaker, stirring up riots among the Jews all over the world. He is a ringleader of the Nazarene sect and even tried to desecrate the temple; so we seized him' (verses 5–6).

Paul denies the charge (verses 11–13). But he says, 'However, I admit that I worship the God of our ancestors as a follower of the Way' (an early description of the Christians) 'which they call a sect' (that is, a sect or party within Judaism):

> I believe everything that is in accordance with the Law and that is written in the Prophets, and I have the same hope in God as these men themselves have, that there will be a resurrection of both the righteous and the wicked. So I strive always to keep my conscience clear before God and man (Acts 24:14–16).

So, says Paul, along with all orthodox Jews of the day, I believe that at the end of time all human beings will be raised from the dead for a day of accountability, a day of judgment, when some will be accounted 'just' or 'righteous' and others 'unjust' or 'wicked'. The just will enter into the life of the age to come, the unjust will be eternally punished by separation from God and all good. I believe that, and this is my reason and motive for striving always to keep a clear conscience.

Now of course that's an unpopular idea, as it always has been. But we expect accountability in all sorts of other ways. When public exams take place we expect there to be a reckoning, a time when our efforts will be assessed. In a workplace we expect there to be accountability. We expect to live in a world where actions have consequences and moral actions have moral consequences. So it is not really all that surprising to believe that there will be a final reckoning for our lives.

And the point Paul is making is this: I know what it is to feel bad or to feel good about something I have done. And in some ways my conscience is a foretaste or indicator of what will happen at the final resurrection. If I feel really bad about something I have done, that really bad feeling is a trailer of a much worse feeling that will come to me in the end. A guilty conscience gives us 'a flash of hell' in the present tense.[4]

And so, says Paul, I take pains to keep a clear conscience, because only if I die with a clear conscience can I die with real grounded confidence that when I awake, I will be accounted clean, just, and righteous and will enter the life of the age to come.

What Paul is doing is making a connection between our present subjective feelings of guilt or innocence and the final objective judgment of our guilt or innocence. That connection is not absolute, for we have seen that we can feel innocent while being guilty and we can feel guilty while being forgiven. Nevertheless, a clear conscience is a reassuring experience, and Paul commends it to us.

To the non-Christian objection to heeding conscience, we must say that a clear conscience is not just an optional way to feel better about myself and life. Without it I cannot with any grounded confidence face death and the final accounting.

A clear conscience honours Christ

The apostle Peter gives another motive for keeping a clear conscience when he wrote to Christians under pressure of persecution. He says to them that they ought not to be frightened, but to honour and revere Christ as Lord, being ready to speak to those who ask about their hope in Christ. They are to do this 'keeping a clear conscience, so that those who speak maliciously against your good behaviour in Christ may be ashamed of their slander' (1 Peter 3:14–16).

A clear conscience brings honour to Christ, because it means that the voice that bears witness to him is backed by a life consistent with that witness.

Warning: a regularly suppressed conscience is a symptom of unreal Christianity

But what about our 'Christian' objection (voiced by Archie) that free forgiveness of all our sins in Christ makes the daily discipline of keeping a clear conscience superfluous? Indeed, that this discipline could even undermine the free grace of God in Christ by making us rely on our clear conscience rather than entirely on what Jesus has done for us?

On the face of it this is a plausible objection and we should find ourselves in some sympathy with it. And yet I believe it to be ultimately misguided and dangerous. It is possible to call myself a Christian without really being a Christian, to be in church without being in Christ. One of the marks of real Christianity is the desire to maintain a clear conscience. If I find myself not caring about the state of my conscience, this is a warning that what I call the grace of God is not really the grace of God at all, but a cheap substitute masquerading as the grace of God (what Dietrich Bonhoeffer famously called 'cheap grace'). If I make a habit of paying no attention to my conscience, then my sorrow at sin (if I show any sorrow at all) will be a worldly sorrow that leads to death, and I set myself on the terrible path we examined in chapter 6, of a gradual and eventually irrevocable hardening of myself against God.

Paul's daily striving to maintain a clear conscience is not a denial of God's grace to him in Christ, but encouraging evidence that he really is a beneficiary of that grace, that he is a real Christian. Or, to put it another way, a clear conscience assists our assurance that we are real Christians and are safe in the hands of God. A guilty conscience, if habitually left untreated, is a warning sign that may suggest that I am not a real Christian after all.

Conscience is not a static thing; it is dynamic.

Conscience is not a static thing; it is dynamic. Inside each of us there is a process going on, either a godly process that leads to salvation or a worldly process that leads to hardening and death.

Facing an honest difficulty: I cannot keep my conscience clean

Dear Paul

I cannot understand how you, of all people, can stand up in public and claim to keep your conscience clean. What do you mean? Before you became a Christian, you actively and viciously persecuted Christians with all the misguided fervour of a fundamentalist religious zealot. You were responsible for killing them. You stood by watching with approval when Stephen was martyred for Christ. How can *you* have a clear conscience about that? It seems to me that either you have a very short memory or you are deluded or you are trying to pull the wool over our (and God's) eyes.

Yours sincerely,

Honest Objector

What exactly does Paul mean by saying that he 'strives always' to keep his conscience clear before God and man? This means being aware of any way in which I have wronged anyone, and doing my best to put it right if I have. It speaks of what I have done or not done, or what I have said – either to them or behind their backs – or not said. It covers how I treat my juniors (my employees, if I am an employer; the staff under me, if I am a manager or in leadership) and my seniors, my neighbours and my work colleagues, my fellow members of a sports club, and others I come into contact with. It covers how I treat my husband or wife, my boyfriend or girlfriend, how I honour my parents, how I care for my children and so on. It is not easy to keep a clear conscience towards all the people with whom I am in any kind of relationship.

But if that's not easy, what about keeping a clear conscience towards God? After all, God looks at my heart! He sees not only what I do and say, but what I want, what I desire, how I feel and what happens in my imagination. I may not have stolen, but God sees the greedy desire for more possessions. I may not have slept with another woman, but God sees the lustful fantasy in the imagination. I may not have acted it out, but God sees the bitter spirit eating me up, the resentment at another's success, the lack of forgiveness against someone who has wronged me. How can I possibly keep a clear conscience before him in my thought life? God knows that it is hard enough to be self-controlled in my actions and words; it is utterly beyond me to be in control of the life of my thoughts and emotions. I cannot do it. And if I think I can, I am self-deceived.

I wonder if you have ever cried out to God in desperation because you have had a glimpse, a horrible glimpse, into the ugly state of your heart. I have. In fact, even as I have written some of this book, I have found myself struggling with all sorts of evil thoughts and desires. I gave up preparing at one stage and just cried out to my heavenly Father for a clean heart.

And Paul knows that. Let us be clear about two things.

First, Paul is most certainly not claiming to have lived a perfect life. Elsewhere he is quite upfront about the terrible things he did to the followers of Jesus before his conversion. He describes himself as having been a blasphemer, a persecutor, an insolent and violent man who had received mercy, upon whom the grace of God had simply overflowed in Christ (1 Timothy 1:13–14). He turned from that old life in repentance, and he trusted in Jesus Christ, the Son of God who loved him and gave himself for him on the cross (Galatians 2:20). So a clear conscience results not from a perfect life, but from repentance and faith.

Secondly – and this is important – Paul is not saying that he became a Christian by repentance and faith but goes on as a Christian by being good. That would be to say that Jesus died in his place for the sins he had committed before his conversion, but that there is no sacrifice available to pay for sins committed afterwards. That would be a recipe for despair.

No, he is saying that he became a Christian by repentance and faith, and he goes on as a Christian by repentance and faith. As Martin Luther famously put it, in the first of his ninety-five theses at Wittenberg, 'The entire life of believers is to be one of repentance.' The start of the Christian life is the shape of the Christian life. I get a clear conscience today the same way I got a cleansed conscience at the start: by turning from known sin and trusting afresh in the blood of Jesus Christ. A clear conscience is a cleansed conscience.

The joy of daily repentance and faith

In this final section I want to spell out the healthy disciplines of consciously repenting daily and deliberately exercising fresh faith in Christ. Or, to put it another way, the joy of keeping a clear conscience before God and people. We will take repentance and faith in turn as they are flip sides of the same coin.

The discipline of regular specific repentance

> When I first began deliberately to repent of particular sins day by day, I would sometimes come to my 'repentance time' and find my mind pretty well blank. Oh, I would always have agreed in theory that I was a sinner. But when push came to shove, I couldn't really think of any specific sins that day!
>
> I found, however, that a short prayer to God by his Holy Spirit to put his finger on sin in my life was speedily answered. And before very long I had no difficulty in thinking of specific things of which I needed to repent.

Do you confess your sins? In many of our churches we say together a shared prayer of corporate repentance for sin, and that is a healthy tradition. But I don't mean just that. What I mean is this: do you, habitually, regularly, even daily, talk openly to God in prayer and say to him, 'Father, I have done this today, and it was wrong. Please forgive me. Father, I said that to so-and-so and I was wrong to say it, or wrong to say it in that way. Please forgive me. Father God, I looked at this today and I was wrong to look at it. Please forgive me. Father, I harboured resentful thoughts today and I was wrong to do that. Please forgive me.'

Do you deliberately, consciously, perhaps even aloud, confess your sins to God? Are there sins that you have not confessed to God, from today, from this week, perhaps from further back, and you carry them as a burden?

My hunch is that most of us confess in theory, but many of us don't in practice. Perhaps some of us who are parents teach our children to say 'sorry' prayers to God, but we neglect to say sorry ourselves. I know that for me it is a habit that has slipped. And it is one I am trying to bring back into my daily routine, so that I end each day with a short time of deliberate intentional repentance before God.

The person quoted in the 'box' at the top of this section is me. Sometimes, to my shame, I look back at the day and find it hard to think of what I need to confess. But generally I find that a few moments' quiet reflection, praying for the Spirit of God to put his finger on things in my heart, yields plenty. As with some of the people of Ezekiel's day, even if there are no very obvious and specific actions or words of which I am aware, there will be 'idols in the heart' (Ezekiel 14:3), things I have set my heart on in the place of God.

A wise old writer said that 'repentance is the vomit of the soul'.[5] This is a shocking and vivid expression for pouring out of us all the disgusting things in our heart. But just as vomiting may be the only way to get rid of something that has poisoned our stomachs, so repentance is the only way to be rid of disgusting things in the heart.

Psalm 32 proclaims to us the joy of repentance. It begins,

Blessed is the one
 whose transgressions are forgiven,
 whose sins are covered.
Blessed is the one
 whose sin the LORD does not count against them
 and in whose spirit is no deceit.
(Psalm 32:1–2)

These first two verses say in three different ways how wonderful (blessed) it is to find forgiveness. And it is a wonderful thing. Our sins are forgiven, covered over by God and not counted against us. As we saw earlier, this forgiveness is possible only because Jesus died for our sin, and our sin was counted against Jesus so that his righteousness could be counted for us.[6]

But the final line is a surprise: ' . . . and in whose spirit is no deceit'. That means the only people who receive the blessing of forgiveness are those who come clean about their sin in open repentance before God. This blessing is for those whose lives are not a cover-up for their sin.

We see what 'deceit' means if we look at the cover-up strategy in the reaction of King Saul in the Old Testament when the prophet Samuel challenges him about not doing what God had told him to do. (You can read the story in 1 Samuel 15.) First, Saul smiles a sweet ingratiating smile at Samuel and says, in effect, 'How nice to see you. I've done what God told me to do.' When Samuel points out that he hasn't, Saul says, 'Ah, well, there's a good reason for that. We're keeping the spirit of the law.' And finally, when Samuel spells out clearly that it was disobedience, Saul says, 'Ah, well, OK, I admit that. But I did do some of what God said and it was the people's fault that we didn't do it all.'[7] It is all cover-up, cover-up and more cover-up. Psalm 32 says there is no blessing for those who cover up their sin. They can never enjoy a clear conscience.

David goes on in the psalm to tell us how miserable he found it when he tried to cover up his sin and soldiered on with a guilty conscience:

> When I kept silent, [that is, about my sin]
>   my bones wasted away
>   through my groaning all day long.
> For day and night
>   your hand was heavy on me;

my strength was sapped
    as in the heat of summer.
(Psalm 32:3–4)

We joke that the Eleventh Commandment is, 'Thou shalt not get found out.' But David's testimony is that not getting caught was a miserable business. Even without God, society shows a recognition of this need to come clean. Some years ago an organization in Los Angeles operated an 'Apology Sound-Off Line', a phone service enabling callers to give sixty-second messages anonymously, confessing their sins. Two hundred callers a day left such confessions. A recent blogger explained, 'When I started this blog, I did so on the premise that I would be painfully honest. I decided that this would be the place, perhaps the only place, where I would bare it all.'

In his strange and in many ways trivial book, *The Secret Lives of Men and Women,* Frank Warren tells how he invited 3,000 people to mail him a personal secret on a self-addressed printed postcard.[8] In the introduction he says, 'People have told me that facing their secret on a postcard and releasing it to a stranger have allowed them to uncover passions, experiences, hopes, regrets, and fears that have been too painful to otherwise acknowledge.'

But unless we confess to God, against whom ultimately our sin is directed, our confession will have no more than a temporary psychological benefit.

Anna Freud was the daughter of Sigmund Freud and a distinguished psychoanalyst in her own right. She was speaking once to a psychiatrist about an elderly lady with a long and troubled psychological history. She ended by saying,

> You know, before we say goodbye to this lady, we should wonder among ourselves not only what to think – we do that all the time! – but what in the world we would want for her. Oh, I don't mean psychotherapy! She's had lots of that. It would take

more years, I suspect, of psycho-analysis than the good Lord has given her. . . . No, she's had her fill of 'us', even if she doesn't know it. . . . This poor old lady doesn't need us at all. . . . What she needs . . . is forgiveness. She needs to make peace with her soul, not talk about her mind. There must be a God, somewhere, to help her, to hear her, to heal her . . . and we certainly aren't the ones who will be of assistance to her in that regard.[9]

A psychiatrist once told me of an occasion when he was asked to assess a church minister who had been unfaithful to his wife. The psychiatrist ended up asking this man, 'Have you ever confessed your sin?' It was perhaps a surprising question from a psychiatrist, but a very perceptive one.

David tells how he finally surrendered:

> Then I acknowledged my sin to you
>   and did not cover up my iniquity.
> I said, 'I will confess
>   my transgressions to the LORD.'
> And you forgave
>   the guilt of my sin.
> (Psalm 32:5)

David abandoned the cover-up. And he discovered that he had a choice: either his sin was covered up by himself (a pointless and painful attempt) or, wonderfully, it could be covered over by God in forgiveness. No sin that is covered up by us can at the same time be covered over by God. This is why confession of sin to God is such a blessing. The moment David confesses, God forgives. As Augustine puts it, 'The word of confession is scarcely out of David's mouth before the wound is healed.'

David is so thrilled with the joy of experienced forgiveness that he exhorts all God's people to do what he has done. 'Therefore let all the faithful [i.e. believers] pray to you while you may be found' (Psalm 32:6). He wants us to find the forgiveness that he experienced. Regular deliberate repentance before God is the first healthy daily discipline for keeping a clear conscience.

Daily repentance is a safeguard against hardness of heart. An old writer compares the hardening of the heart to the freezing of water on a lake:

> As water, when it begins to freeze, will not endure anything, no not so much as the weight of a pin upon it, but after a while will bear the weight of a cart; even so at the beginning, the heart being tender, trembles at the least sin, and will not bear with any one; but when it once gives way to sins against conscience, it becomes so frozen that it can endure any sin, and so becomes more and more hard.[10]

Repenting with others

Sometimes repenting of particular sins in the presence of others can help us come to know in experience that these particular sins are forgiven.

I want to pause a moment and ask, how can we know that a particular sin has been forgiven? What I mean is this: in theory we can know because the gospel tells us that 'if we confess our sins, [God] is faithful and just and will forgive us our sins and purify us from all unrighteousness' (1 John 1:9). But how do we come to experience in practice the joy of knowing our sins forgiven?

In his book *Prayer Life: How Your Personality Affects the Way You Pray*, Pablo Martinez addresses this question as a psychiatrist. He writes, 'Some people . . . do not feel this relieving and soothing effect of confession, even though their prayer has been genuine. "I know that God has forgiven me, but I do not feel it inside." Why?'[11]

Sometimes, he says, the problem is that we will not forgive ourselves. But he goes on to write that sometimes it can be helpful to confess to someone else. This is not so much confessing to them as 'confessing to God in the company of another person'. This provides 'a very healthy amount of objectivity that contributes to dissipating psychological doubts' in a way that private and silent confession may not do.

This may be why James exhorts us to 'confess your sins to each other and pray for each other so that you may be healed' (James 5:16). Martinez writes,

> From the emotional point of view, this is important because the injuries heal over much more rapidly when someone intimately knows about our sin and has prayed with us and for us. Many patients have expressed their deep gratitude to me because in my office they have been able to open up their heart and pour out those secrets of their life that they had never before shared with anyone else. The tears shed in the company of another have a therapeutic potential far greater than the emotions expressed in solitude. Tears in solitude can become embittering to the soul, tears in company are almost always soothing to the broken heart.[12]

In his excellent book *Captured by a Better Vision*,[13] Tim Chester also writes of the blessing of accountability and of open confession in the context of Christian trust, as sinners together before God.

But having said this, we must never make the mistake of thinking a fellow Christian can act towards us like an Old Testament priest, being an intermediary *between* us and God. There is one priest, and one alone, who can be our mediator with God and assure us of forgiveness: the Lord Jesus Christ, our great High Priest, and we need no other. As an old poem puts it:

> One Priest alone can pardon me,
> Or bid me, 'Go in peace';
> Can breathe that word *'Absolvo te'*
> And make these heart-throbs cease;
> My soul has heard His priestly voice;
> It said, 'I bore thy sins – Rejoice.'[14]

So if we do sometimes confess to God in the presence of other Christians, we do not look to them to be mediators between us and God. The most they can do is strengthen our faith in the cross of Christ.

Repenting includes keeping a clear conscience towards those we have wronged

Repentance before God, if it is real, will always be accompanied by repentance towards any people we are conscious of having wronged. I will examine my life regularly to ask whether there are any ways in which I have mistreated people – by my manner, by the words I have spoken about them behind their backs, by unfair judgments of their motives, by my use of money, in my professional or business relationships, in marriage and in the family. And where God convicts me that I have done wrong, I will do all in my power to make restitution.

One of the most vivid examples of this in the New Testament is the greedy, corrupt tax-farmer Zacchaeus, who was so changed by Jesus that he publicly pledged not only to give back what he had defrauded people of, but to give more and more (Luke 19:1–10).

A friend once told me of a man called David who had done very well running a water-bottling business in Wales. And then in London he came to faith in Christ. David wrote to the tax authorities, telling them that he had defrauded them of £300,000 in unpaid tax, and could he please pay it now. That is repentance. (In the end the Inland Revenue wrote back saying that they could trace unpaid tax of only £75,000, so they'd be happy with that!) David took pains to have a clear conscience towards others. We too should do likewise.

Regular personal application of the blood of Christ

We've seen that repentance and faith are the two sides of becoming a Christian and going on being a Christian. So far as keeping a clear conscience is concerned, faith means trusting God's promise that Jesus Christ's death on the cross pays for all our sins. It means taking the objective truth of Jesus' death for us and applying it to our subjective experience (as we saw in chapter 7). This is so important that we are going to close with it by way of emphasis.

It is by trusting in the death of Jesus that we experience afresh the subjective assurance of the forgiveness of our sins. In the metaphorical language of the Bible, this is like thinking again of the blood of Christ that covers all our sin. In one sense, objectively, this is not necessary. Once we became a Christian, all our sins – past, present and future – were covered by the blood of Christ for all eternity. But in terms of our subjective experience, our confidence, our feelings of joyful assurance, we do need to feel afresh the blood of Christ applied to our sin again and again.

I find it a help to use (and sing) some of the words from old hymns that celebrate this truth. One of my favourites is William Cowper's hymn, which begins,

> There is a fountain filled with blood
> Drawn from Immanuel's veins
> And sinners plunged beneath that flood
> Lose all their guilty stains.

The graphic imagery is a bit strong for some soft modern sensibilities, but its theology is exactly right, and we would do well to learn to make use of such vivid Bible metaphorical language ourselves. I love to sing this hymn and meditate on the word 'all', in the words 'lose *all* their guilty stains', consciously applying this truth to the particular sinful desire, affection, word or deed that I am confessing. It helps me trust afresh that the blood of Jesus really does cover all my sin. As the old Puritan Richard Sibbes put it: 'Be always under the sunshine of the gospel.'[15]

And then I experience afresh the joy of a cleansed conscience and feel that, without self-righteousness, without self-deception,

I really can say, 'My conscience is clean; I have nothing on my conscience.' May God make this true in your experience and in your life too.

Questions for personal study or discussion

1. Do you deliberately and intentionally keep a clear conscience towards God and people day by day? If you don't, think about why not.

2. How does a guilty conscience undermine any Christian assurance you may have that you are in the right with God?

3. How does keeping a clear conscience bring honour to Christ?

4. How does our attitude to conscience function as a warning light to alert us to inauthentic Christianity?

5. Have you ever tried to keep a clear conscience simply by being good? Did it work?

6. Do you confess your sins deliberately, specifically, intentionally and regularly? If not, why not try developing the habit of doing this? If you cannot think of specific sins to confess, pause a moment and pray that God will put his finger on something, perhaps an attitude of the heart.

7. Have you experienced the relief and joy of knowing that a particular sin is forgiven?

8. Have you ever found it helpful to confess a sin in the presence of another Christian (or Christians)? How has this helped? How can we do this without falling into the trap of thinking we can do this only with 'special' people who somehow help us get access to God?

9. Is there anyone you need to be reconciled to, by actually doing something to put right some way you have wronged them?

10. Have you learned the habit of consciously reminding yourself of the blood of Christ that covers not just your sin in general, but a particular and specific sin that troubles you?

Notes

1. Paul says something very similar in Acts 23:1: 'I have fulfilled my duty to God in all good conscience to this day'; and to Timothy in 2 Timothy 1:3: 'I thank God, whom I serve, as my ancestors did, with a clear conscience.'
2. Article on 'Conscience', in G. Kittel (ed.), *Theological Dictionary of the New Testament* (Eerdmans, 2006).
3. See the introduction.
4. See chapter 4.
5. Thomas Brooks, *Precious Remedies Against Satan's Devices*. I am grateful to Robin Weekes for this quotation.
6. See Romans 4:4–8.
7. I have paraphrased 1 Samuel 15:13–15 and 20.

8. Frank Warren, *The Secret Lives of Men and Women* (HarperCollins, 2007).

9. Quoted in Johann Christoph Arnold, *The Lost Art of Forgiving* (Plough Publishing House, 1998), p. 120.

10. Richard Sibbes, *The Tender Heart* (Banner of Truth, 2011), pp. 29–30.

11. Pablo Martinez, *Prayer Life: How Your Personality Affects the Way You Pray* (Paternoster, 2002), p. 98 (the section on pp. 95–102 is insightful and helpful on this).

12. Martinez, *Prayer Life,* p. 100.

13. Tim Chester, *Captured by a Better Vision: Living Porn-free* (IVP, 2010).

14. Andrew Atherstone, *'I Absolve You': Private Confession and the Church of England* (Latimer Trust, 2005), p. 39.

15. Sibbes, *The Tender Heart,* p. 51.

APPENDIX: FOUR SNAPSHOTS FROM HISTORY

THIS APPENDIX is for those who are interested to read about some of the debates that have taken place in history about conscience. These four snapshots are far from comprehensive, but they will give us a flavour of some of the angles from which people have approached this subject.

Snapshot 1: The Middle Ages. Conscience as universal moral knowledge

Christian theologians in the Middle Ages thought a lot about conscience and its role in Christian living. Often they drew a distinction between knowing general principles of right and wrong and the application of those principles to particular choices in life.[1] Sometimes they considered our knowledge of first principles to be mainly an intellectual thing; sometimes they included with this 'the drive towards good', a 'push' or 'pull' that affects our will and emotions so that we don't want to do wrong and we desire to do right. Indeed, 'without the desire to put the dictates or conscience into play, conscience is little more than an extension of the imagination; that is, through conscience we would picture how to behave to reach the good, but not sense that we should do what we picture.'[2]

So, for example, Bonaventure[3] suggested that all human beings have an unerring knowledge of the general principles of right and wrong but sometimes make mistakes in applying those principles to particular decisions. He did recognize that our consciences are dynamic; they develop and mature or worsen over time. We need to work at improving the exercise of our consciences. Good behaviour improves our consciences, and our consciences are damaged by bad behaviour. Conscience both directs our behaviour and also changes with the results of our behaviour. For example, if we have done something wrong, we naturally want to justify ourselves, and so our conscience shifts so as to make our bad behaviour seem acceptable.

Bonaventure grappled with the question of whether conscience can ever be extinguished in the life of a wicked person. He recognized that it can be damaged by blindness (or ignorance, which sees evil as good), by pleasure (or what we would call being carried away by passions), and by moral perversity or hardness of heart (a deliberate suppression of conscience). But he suggested that even in 'the damned' who reach the point where they can never turn towards good (never repent), the conscience is not extinguished completely, but can still 'sting and murmur' against evil, which is a kind of punishment in advance.

Thomas Aquinas (perhaps the greatest theologian of the medieval church) stressed the calm rational aspect of conscience, an infallible disposition of the mind by which we know basic principles of behaviour.[4] We see his influence in the definition of conscience in the *Catechism of the Catholic Church*: 'Conscience is a judgment of reason whereby the human person recognizes the moral quality of a concrete act that he is going to perform, is in the process of performing, or has already performed.'[5]

Like Bonaventure, Aquinas asked how conscience functions in evil people. His answer was that there is a distinction between two kinds of people. On the one hand is what he called 'the intemperate man', a self-indulgent person whose whole life is driven by pleasure and whose vice is habitual. On the other hand is 'the incontinent man' (that is, in the old sense of morally lacking self-control), who knows what he ought to do and wants to do it, but is driven off course by the force of passions. But unlike the first man, this one's failures are 'occasional and episodic', like having epileptic seizures from time to time. His failures are out of character and they do not reflect his overall direction of life.[6]

For both Bonaventure and Aquinas, conscience can be damaged but not destroyed. In all of us there is some irreducible grounding of knowledge about right and wrong, and however much we may ignore the promptings of our consciences, this knowledge remains. If we asked them, 'Is conscience the voice of God?' they would, I think, have answered, 'Yes, and no: yes, fundamentally, in our irreducible and sure knowledge of right and wrong; but no, in that we sometimes misapply this knowledge in our judgment of particular cases.'

This view may be summed up by this quotation from the *Catechism of the Catholic Church*:

> Deep within his conscience man discovers a law which he has not laid upon himself but which he must obey. Its voice, ever calling him to love and do what is good and to avoid evil, sounds in his heart at the right moment. . . . For man has in his heart a law inscribed by God. . . . His conscience is man's most secret core and his sanctuary. There he is alone with God whose voice echoes in his depths.'[7]

Snapshot 2: From Luther to the Puritans. Conscience as guide to personal virtue under the law of God

The mainstream medieval theologians did not generally have much time for what we might call 'the weakness of the will', the utter inability of human beings to follow the dictates of conscience without the free grace of God in Christ and the motions of the Holy Spirit in the heart. We have seen that it was Martin Luther who rediscovered this truth. For Luther, the conscience has a tremendous role in condemnation. Far from being a quiet, rational and reliable guide to godly behaviour, the conscience, being guilty, shows me that I am utterly condemned and without hope in the presence of a holy God. My conscience does indeed show me right and wrong, but I am utterly powerless in myself to do right and must cast myself on the mercy of the Saviour.

For Luther, the conscience

> rages and cries out, it despairs, shudders and trembles, it may become restless, anxious and fearful. These emotions are caused by man's experience of God's wrath, and by the law's judging and punishing activity. The conscience thus becomes the sphere in which humanity experiences the reality of sin and corruption. It encapsulates the individual's inner nucleus as he or she stands before God; through the conscience humankind in its totality is addressed by the condemning law.[8]

Luther's big contribution was in seeing that conscience is much more than an aspect of moral reasoning; it speaks to me as a whole person and judges me, not just my actions. My conscience is about my heart. Luther's insight led in two directions. First, and healthily, it opened the way for the role of conscience to be tied in to issues of character and virtue, rather than just to the rights and wrongs of particular actions. By the gracious ministry of the Holy Spirit within me, writing the law of God within the heart so that I begin at the deepest level of human personhood to want to do it, God begins to enable me to do what my conscience says I should do.

The Puritans developed this emphasis on conscience and virtue. Conscience played a significant role in their understanding of living the Christian life. It is a voice within me that is the echo of God's law outside me, and therefore a voice to which I should pay close attention. One of the most influential of the Puritan writers was William Perkins, who wrote a whole treatise on conscience. For the Puritans, conscience 'stands over us, addressing us with an absoluteness of authority which we did not give it and which we cannot take from it. To personify conscience and treat it as God's watchman and spokesman in the soul is not, therefore, a mere flight of fancy, it is a necessity of human experience.' They even called it 'God's deputy and vice-regent within us'. It is God's courtroom within us.[9]

Snapshot 3: From Luther to Kant and Ryle. Conscience as individual authority independent of the law of God

However, in time, Luther's emphasis on conscience and the heart of a person was taken in another direction. When the prevailing intellectual culture ceased to believe in universal moral laws,

> the emphasis on conscience as a personal faculty increased. If there are not universal laws of behaviour, each person must have an individual faculty for determining how he or she should act. Although an individual may listen to others' viewpoints, the individual's faculty of conscience is the final judge for the individual.[10]

Whereas the Puritans thought about conscience within a strong framework of reliable and universal moral laws revealed in the Bible, these philosophers treated conscience as a faculty of human autonomy in the absence of universal truth. So Immanuel Kant speaks eloquently of a man or woman's conscience as an 'internal court' in each individual, with an authority, 'watching over the law in him' (note: not the law of God outside him, but the personal 'law in him', what is right for him).

This is what Kant wrote:

Consciousness of an *internal court* in man ('before which his thoughts accuse or excuse one another') is conscience. Every man has a conscience and finds himself observed, threatened, and, in general, kept in awe (respect coupled with fear) by an internal judge; and this authority watching over the law in him is not something that he himself (voluntarily) makes, but something incorporated in his being. It follows him like his shadow when he plans to escape. He can indeed stun himself or put himself to sleep by pleasures and distractions, but he cannot help coming to himself or waking up from time to time; and when he does, he hears at once its fearful voice. He can at most, in extreme depravity, bring himself to *heed* it no longer, but he still cannot help *hearing* it.

Now this original intellectual and (since it is the thought of duty) moral predisposition called *conscience* is peculiar in that, although its business is a business of man with himself, a man constrained by his reason sees himself constrained to carry it on as at the bidding of another person [that is to say, we must think of conscience almost as if it were another person alongside us].[11]

Kant's idea of conscience is of an 'internal court' and he represents a turning away from taking seriously the objective truth of God. For Kant, conscience becomes a merely subjective and individual guide.

In the twentieth century the philosopher Gilbert Ryle took this trajectory to its logical conclusion.[12] His essay 'Conscience and Moral Convictions' is one of the seminal twentieth-century philosophical essays on conscience. Ryle regards conscience as a private monitor, which exercises authority over me as an individual but does not and cannot relate to any wider authority that might, for example, also exercise authority over you. 'It is absurd to say, "My conscience says that *you* ought to do this or ought not to have done that" '. For Ryle, 'conscience is the self-application by a particular person of moral convictions he or she holds'.

Both of these take conscience as an individual, subjective and internal faculty that can exercise at best a personal authority over an individual. It must be obeyed as the voice of the god within, but not as the voice of an objective God outside, a God who rules others as well as myself.

Snapshot 4: Sigmund Freud. Conscience as parental and cultural legacy[13]

Our final snapshot is the influential twentieth-century psycho-analyst Sigmund Freud, whose argument tends to undermine the idea that conscience could ever in any way be the voice of God. Freud famously analysed the human person into three parts ('the psychic apparatus of human beings'): the id, the ego and the superego. The id is present at birth in all of us and broadly speaking represents our instincts (much as with animal instincts, such as the instinct to self-preservation). The ego ('I' or my self) develops from the id under the influence of the external world, and particularly the world of the parent(s) as it impacts the world of the child. This is how 'I' develop a distinct personal identity.

But what is significant for our thinking is the superego. Freud describes it like this:

> The long period of childhood, during which the growing human being lives in dependence on his parents, leaves behind it as a precipitate the formation in his ego of a special agency in which this parental influence is prolonged. It has received the name of superego. In so far as this superego is differentiated from the ego or is opposed to it, it constitutes a third power which the ego must take into account.[14]

That is to say, all through childhood, a boy or girl absorbs from parents, from other adults, from the culture in which they are immersed, from their schooling and so on, a whole raft of values, customs and assumptions about right and wrong. Although they develop their own identity (the ego), they cannot entirely leave behind this cultural baggage they have taken on board themselves. Some of it is inevitably left behind as 'a precipitate' (like what is left after some chemical processes). Freud includes in this not just parental values, but things like racial assumptions and national values.

This superego remains in me as 'something like a repository of authority that has been internalised' within me. It changes gradually over time in response to new personal and cultural influences. But I cannot make a clean break from it. Freud regards the conscience as pretty much equivalent to the superego in its role of passing judgment on my actions. The ego cannot be completely autonomous and just go and live its own life. The superego 'observes the ego, gives it orders, judges it, and threatens it with punishments, exactly like the parents whose place it has taken'.

The lines that conscience draws are therefore, according to Freud, not absolute or universal at all but entirely cultural. They are no more than 'the interiorization of the norms of parents and society'.[15] And my bad feelings when I have a guilty conscience have nothing at all to do with objective guilt, but everything to do with the child's fear of loss of love when he or she disobeys the parent. Conscience is no more than 'an emotional buzzer'[16] that sounds when I branch out and do (or propose to do) something different from my parents and their culture. Conscience is a cultural legacy imposed on me and from whose repressive influence I would do well to break free. It has no moral content.

Notes

1. For curious reasons they sometimes used the word *synderesis* (or *synteresis*) for our knowledge of first principles of moral action, and

reserved the word *conscience* for the application of those principles. See Douglas C. Langston, *Conscience and Other Virtues* (Pennsylvania State University Press, 2001), p. 9, and 'Synderesis', in F. L. Cross and E. A. Livingstone (eds.), *The Oxford Dictionary of the Christian Church* (OUP, 2005).

2. Quoted in Langston, *Conscience*, p. 31.

3. Bonaventure lived c. 1221–74 and was a prominent Franciscan theologian based in Paris.

4. See Langston, *Conscience*, pp. 39–47.

5. Quoted in Langston, *Conscience*, p. 109.

6. See Langston, *Conscience*, pp. 44–47.

7. Quoted in Langston, *Conscience*, p. 111.

8. Philip Bosman, *Conscience in Philo and Paul* (Mohr Siebeck, 2003), p. 21.

9. See J. I. Packer, *Among God's Giants: The Puritan Vision of the Christian Life* (Kingsway, 1991), p. 145.

10. Langston, *Conscience*, p. 8.

11. Quoted in Langston, *Conscience*, p. 82.

12. See Langston, *Conscience*, pp. 91–98.

13. Langston, *Conscience*, pp. 87–91.

14. Quoted in Langston, *Conscience*, p. 88.

15. 'Conscience', in Sinclair B. Ferguson and David F. Wright (eds.), *New Dictionary of Theology* (IVP, 1988).

16. Langston, *Conscience*, p. 2.

AFTERWORD:
WHY I WROTE THIS BOOK

I BEGAN WORKING ON this book when I was preaching through Romans 14 and 15. Although the word *conscience* is not used there, the idea and principle of conscience is central to the argument. But when reading around the passages, I could find very little in contemporary or recent Christian writing about the subject. I found a slightly eccentric book dating from 1950 and a helpful booklet from 1964, but very little else. I knew from studies of church history that the Puritans spoke much about conscience, and that some felt that they veered towards an unhelpful morbid introspection. But it seemed to me that we had gone to the opposite extreme of neglecting conscience almost altogether.

Conscience is a subjective experience that ought to be rooted in objective truth. In some of our Christian circles, it seems to me that we have rightly emphasized the objective truth but carelessly neglected to enquire into the subjective experience. (In other circles, of course, we have gone overboard with subjective experience and failed to anchor it to objective truth.)

Perhaps the most important reason why I have written this book is to urge and encourage you to make a careful watchfulness of your conscience an integral part of your Christian life.

Writing about the Puritans and their teaching about conscience, J. I. Packer says,

> A good conscience is a tender conscience. The consciences of the godless may be so calloused that they scarcely ever act at all; but the healthy Christian conscience ... is constantly in operation, listening for God's voice in his word, seeking to discern his will in everything, active in self-watch and self-judgement. The healthy Christian knows his frailty and always suspects and distrusts himself, lest sin and Satan should be ensnaring him unawares; therefore he regularly grills himself before God, scrutinizing his deeds and motives and ruthlessly condemning himself when he finds within himself moral deficiency and dishonesty ...
>
> The healthy Christian is not necessarily the extravert, ebullient Christian, but the Christian who has a sense of God's presence stamped deep upon his soul, who trembles at God's word, who lets it dwell in him richly by constant meditation upon it, and who tests and reforms his life daily in response to it.[1]

My aim in this book has been to get you thinking about conscience. I hope you have taken your conscience out of the cupboard, dusted it off, brought it back into daily life and discovered its power to do you good. I hope and pray that this book has helped.

You may like to use this prayer as you look to the future.

> Almighty Creator God, who is my heavenly Father, you see into the depths of my heart. You know not only what I have done and said, but all my mixed motives, my disordered desires, my misdirected delights. On my own I have no hope of standing clean in your presence. Thank you for your Son the Lord Jesus Christ, who died to cleanse me from every sin. By your Spirit may I know day by day in living experience the joy of a conscience cleansed by the blood of Christ. By your grace help

me to take pains always to keep a clear conscience towards God
and people. Help me finally to come to my death strengthened
by the joy of a cleansed conscience.

For Jesus' sake, Amen.

Notes

1. J. I. Packer, *Among God's Giants: The Puritan Vision of the Christian Life*
   (Kingsway, 1991), pp. 151–152.

SCRIPTURE INDEX

MORE RESOURCES FROM P&R

Barbara Duguid turns to the writings of John Newton to teach us God's purpose for our failure and guilt—and to help us adjust our expectations of ourselves. Her empathetic, honest approach lifts our focus from our own performance back to the God who is bigger than our failures—and who uses them for his glory. Rediscover how God's extravagant grace makes the gospel once again feel like the good news it truly is!

"Take this book to heart. It will sustain you for the long haul, long after the hyped-up panaceas and utopias fail."
> —**David Powlison,** Faculty Member at the Christian Counseling and Educational Foundation

"We need more and more books like this that remind us that the focus of the Christian faith is not the life of the Christian, but Christ."
> —**Tullian Tchividjian,** Pastor of Coral Ridge Presbyterian Church, Author of *Jesus + Nothing = Everything*

MORE RESOURCES FROM P&R

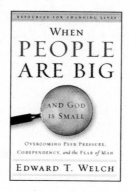

"Need people less. Love people more. That's the author's challenge. . . . He's talking about a tendency to hold other people in awe, to be controlled and mastered by them, to depend on them for what God alone can give. . . . [Welch] proposes an antidote: the fear of God . . . the believer's response to God's power, majesty and not least his mercy."
   —*Dallas Morning News*

"Refreshingly biblical . . . brimming with helpful, readable, practical insight."
   —**John MacArthur,** President of The Master's College and Seminary

"Ed Welch is a good physician of the soul. This book is enlightening, convicting, and encouraging. I highly recommend it."
   —**Jerry Bridges,** Author of *Trusting God*